This book is dedicated to my family, Ryan, Niki, and Mikaila, who encourage and inspire me.

Acknowledgments

A special thanks to Mitzi Koontz, Acquisitions Editor, for her vision and support with this project and to Kate Shoup, Project and Copy Editor, for her expertise and assistance. It is a pleasure to work with such dedicated professionals. Thanks also to the many others who had a hand in producing this book.

About the Author

Carol A. Silvis is the author of several books, including *Job Hunting After 50, 101 Ways to Make Yourself Indispensable at Work, 100% Externship Success*, and *General Office Procedures*, all available through Cengage Learning. Other publications include "Time Management and Organization for Writers" (*2012 Writers Market*), a dozen creative non-fiction stories and inspirational pieces published in national magazines, and more than 40 articles published in various newsletters.

Ms. Silvis has been interviewed by Yahoo.com, AARP online, CBSMoneywatch.com, ABCNews.com, and *Writer's Digest*. She has also appeared on Cornerstone TV, HMC-TV, and WIUP-TV.

Carol has a master's degree in education and has trained adults in how to get a job, keep and enjoy their job, and get ahead. She gives workshops and seminars for schools, businesses, professional organizations, and libraries on a wide range of business topics.

Carol is the president of Pennwriters, Inc., received the 2008 Meritorious Service Award, and was the 2005 and 2007 Conference Coordinator.

Visit her website, www.carolsilvis.com, and blog, www.carolsilvis.blogspot.com.

101 Ways to Connect with Your Customers, Chiefs, and Co-Workers

CAROL A. SILVIS, M.ED.

Cengage Learning PTR

CENGAGE Learning

Professional • Technical • Reference

Australia, Brazil, Japan, Korea, Mexico, Singapore, Spain, United Kingdom, United States

CENGAGE
Learning·

Professional • Technical • Reference

**101 Ways to Connect
with Your Customers,
Chiefs, and Co-Workers**
Carol A. Silvis, M.Ed.

**Publisher and
General Manager,
Cengage Learning PTR:**
Stacy L. Hiquet

**Associate Director
of Marketing:**
Sarah Panella

**Manager of
Editorial Services:**
Heather Talbot

**Senior Marketing
Manager:**
Mark Hughes

**Senior Acquisitions
Editor:**
Mitzi Koontz

**Project and Copy
Editor:**
Kate Shoup

Interior Layout:
Shawn Morningstar

Cover Designer:
Luke Fletcher

Proofreader:
Mike Beady

Printed in the United
States of America
1 2 3 4 5 6 7 16 15 14

For product information and technology
assistance, contact us at
**Cengage Learning Customer and Sales Support, 1-
800-354-9706.**

For permission to use material from this
text or product, submit all requests online at
cengage.com/permissions.

Further permissions questions can be
e-mailed to **permissionrequest@cengage.com.**

All trademarks are the property of their respective owners.

Library of Congress Control Number: 2013955971
ISBN-13: 978-1-305-09762-9
ISBN-10: 1-305-09762-9

Cengage Learning PTR
20 Channel Center Street
Boston, MA 02210
USA

Cengage Learning is a leading provider of customized
learning solutions with office locations around the
globe, including Singapore, the United Kingdom,
Australia, Mexico, Brazil, and Japan. Locate your
local office at: **international.cengage.com/region.**

Cengage Learning products are represented in Canada
by Nelson Education, Ltd.

For your lifelong learning solutions, visit **cengageptr.com.**
Visit our corporate Web site at **cengage.com.**

Contents

Introduction

This book is composed of 101 excellent ways to connect with customers, chiefs, and co-workers. No matter where you work, your job will probably require at least some connection with other people.

The first three chapters of this book focus on interaction with customers and chiefs, necessitating good communication skills and a professional work ethic. Chapters 4–6 focus on building positive work relationships with chiefs and co-workers. Chapters 7–9 focus on interaction with customers, chiefs, and co-workers. These chapters contain strategies to help you engage successfully with others with whom you associate in a variety of situations.

The tips and suggestions in this book encourage, motivate, and guide the reader in building positive work relationships and contributing to a positive environment.

PART I

INTERACTING WITH CUSTOMERS AND CHIEFS

1

COMMUNICATE EFFECTIVELY WITH CUSTOMERS

In this book, you will find 101 ways to connect with people you deal with in the workplace, whether internally or externally. Communication is a major part of connecting. By using these 101 strategies, you will do your part to build a more harmonious workplace and to attract and keep customers.

No matter your position, if you are employed, you will deal with people to some extent. The more you associate with different personalities, work habits, managerial styles, and the like, the more imperative good communication skills become. These 101 ways of connecting with people can help you advance in your career.

1.

Do Not Lie or Cheat When Selling Products or Providing Services

Have you ever dealt with a company you felt sold an inferior product or service? Have you done business with an organization and later discovered its mission was unscrupulous? If so, how did this make you feel? Misled? Cheated? Angry? Either of these scenarios would probably be enough to turn you away from doing business with a company. If you have been taken advantage of by a company, remember how you felt afterward when you provide customer service to others. To ensure they don't wind up feeling the same way you did, take care to treat people honestly and fairly. People understandably react negatively when they are misled or cheated. If they feel they were sold shoddy products or were provided inferior service, they will hardly be satisfied. It is important not to misrepresent the facts, even if it means losing a current sale.

Do your best to provide products and services that will keep customers satisfied. They may become return customers. They might even tell their friends about your company's fine products and services.

Have you dealt with a particular salesperson you suspected was less than honest or was hiding something from you about the products or services he represented? It is a good bet you will not only avoid that salesman in the future but will also avoid the company. After all, if that company continues to employ him, it sends a negative message. Either the employer does not know what the salesman is doing or the company knows but allows him to continue. Either way, the company's reputation is undermined, because customers expect an organization to hire honest employees. Keep your reputation above reproach.

Lies and cheating damage your reputation. Keep your word when providing services. A broken promise damages integrity and causes the customer to lose confidence in you, your products, and your company. Even one misstatement or misstep can have devastating consequences on your customer service, no matter how innocent on your part. Once a customer loses faith in you, everything you tell him from that point forward will become suspect.

Customers have different needs and wants. Your company may be in a position to serve those needs. Be visible and accessible to determine what customers want and need. Form a relationship with them based on honesty to gain their trust and repeat business. Begin by identifying what customers need, figuring out how you can provide for them, and then doing it. As you offer your services, remember the "Golden Rule": Treat customers as you would like to be treated.

It is important to understand what you are selling to a customer. How can you provide honest, complete information to a customer if you have incomplete data or are unfamiliar with your products? Make it your business to know everything there is to know about your products if it is feasible to do so. Try the product, study it, read the research on it, and seek answers to your questions. Do the same with the services you provide. Use them.

Demonstrate your commitment to your company by becoming an expert on as many products your company makes as you can. Of course, if you work in retail, that may be impossible. If that is the case, know where to find the appropriate information on products. If it is impossible to become familiar with all of your products because of the variety and volume, be as confident as feasible.

When you know your products and services inside and out, you can provide correct information without exaggerating or second-guessing. If you do not know the answer to a customer's question, refrain from giving a random answer just to silence the customer. Find the correct answer or ask someone who knows.

It is time-consuming and inefficient to constantly recruit new customers, so you must keep the ones you have by providing the best quality products and services. Be upfront with the customers during each and every dealing you have with them.

Be helpful even when there is no immediate return for you, such as when a customer wants a product you do not have. Can you recommend another company that does have the product? Someone you help today may return when she needs something your company provides. She may even recommend others to you. The success of a business depends on repeat customers.

As changes are made to your products and services, stay up to date so you will be ready to answer your customer's questions. Keep in mind that customers are giving you their hard-earned money and/or time. They deserve to deal with someone who has a mastery of the item they want or the work they need completed. Continually update yourself on the latest changes in your field so you can determine if your products and services are meeting the highest standards.

With any product or service, a problem may occasionally arise. Do all you can to create a positive perception of your company and its products and services. Every so often, a customer may feel she is being taken advantage of even if it is not true. What can you do to assure her your company wants to resolve the situation to her satisfaction? Handle it quickly, as outlined in tip 3.

Word of mouth is a powerful way to gain new customers, as people generally trust the opinions of people they know. The same holds true for losing customers because of negative comments.

Create quality products and services and become an expert on them. Give the customer honest information.

2.
Do Not Pass the Buck

Have you ever called attention to a problem and had the person you complained to brush you off? Have you called a company only to get caught up in an endless loop of extensions that led nowhere? Were you eventually hung up on? Did you ever feel a lack of accountability or organization among a company's employees? How about getting the feeling the company operated like some secret service organization, where no one admitted to knowing what was going on or how to respond to questions and problems? If you answered yes to any of these questions, you know that situations like these cause annoyance at the very least.

"Passing the buck" is how customers describe when no one will take responsibility for solving their problems. These customers accuse company personnel of pushing their concerns off on someone else, who then pushes the concerns off on another person, in an endless cycle that leaves customers frustrated and with unresolved problems. After talking to a number of company representatives who will not or cannot help, many customers resolve to never do business with that company again. In addition, they may pursue other avenues, including legal paths.

Although there are times when it is necessary to route a customer to another extension or direct him to someone else, doing so more than once is likely to make for an unhappy customer. To avoid misdirecting customers, be sure you know your company's policy for handling complaints and the personnel who provide that service so you can connect the customer to the correct person the first time around. All employees should know proper procedures. The fewer times you hand off a customer to another employee, the less frustration that customer is likely to experience.

It is easy to push problems and complaints off on someone else, but before you consider doing so, imagine how the customer will feel. Is there any way you can handle the problem without referring her to someone else? If you absolutely must direct the customer to someone else, do you know the proper procedure? Are you sure the person to whom you are transferring the customer can and will handle the problem? Even when it is the correct choice to refer the customer to another person or department, you should offer as much assistance as possible to ensure customer satisfaction. Take care to direct the customer to the correct person the first time to prevent her from being bounced from person to person.

Accept responsibility for resolving customer problems if you have the ability and it is within the scope of your authority. If the customer's request is beyond your responsibility, offer to be a liaison between the customer and the person who can best handle the problem. Never leave a customer suspended. If you are not sure who is best able to help the customer, offer to contact the customer after you find out rather than keep her waiting or referring her to the wrong person.

When it is necessary to direct a customer to someone else, be sure that person is able and willing to help the customer. Otherwise, the customer may feel she is getting the runaround. Some customers may need some hand-holding to get from one place to another. Be willing to go above and beyond to assist them. If the customer is on the phone, tell her you are transferring the call and then give her the name and extension of the transfer. If the customer is with you in person, walk with her to the proper department rather than pointing and sending her on her way.

A customer's frustration will mount quickly if she gets the impression her concerns are being brushed aside. When that happens, you may lose not only the current sale, but also future sales from that customer. Do your part to provide the best customer service possible.

When a complaint is lodged, focus on the solution, but learn as much as you can about the problem to prevent a similar incident in the future. If the problem is not your fault but you are the one who is called on to resolve it, never blame your co-workers or the supervisor, even when justified. Your main concern should be satisfying the customer, not placing blame. Apologize and offer to help find a solution or to connect the customer with the person who can provide one.

If someone else is to blame for a problem and you are in a position of authority and need to correct that person, speak to him privately rather than bringing it up in front of the customer. If you are to blame, apologize and work on a solution.

Never give a customer the runaround. Provide assistance or find someone who can.

3.

Seek Equitable Solutions to Problems

When a customer complains to you about a problem, assume the complaint is legitimate and set about working on an equitable solution. How do you arrive at an equitable solution? You will need to gather all the facts, brainstorm ideas, and choose the solution that is fair to the customer and will satisfy him while maintaining integrity and profitability for your company.

Address problems immediately upon hearing from the customer. Delay may cause the customer to think you are not willing to help him. No matter the problem, apologize when he is dissatisfied and offer to help him file a claim.

Listen to what the customer wants. Recognize what he needs. Can you do what he asks? If so, respond immediately for a quick, satisfying resolution. If you cannot do as asked, how far apart are you and the customer on ideas for a resolution? By figuring out this gap, you will have important criteria to develop an alternative solution.

Treat each customer's problem as an individual case. After all, it is unique to him even if you have handled similar cases.

After gathering information from the customer, review it. If you do not understand what the customer is saying or what he wants, ask for clarifications on ambiguous points. Repeat the information as you understand it. Assuming you know what the customer wants without clarifying the details could cause additional problems. Add your perspective to what the customer has told you. Try to explain the problem as you understand it and the proposed solution in a way that will not make the customer feel stupid or inferior.

Using plain language, tell the customer what you can and cannot do about his problem. Clear, easy-to-understand language prevents misunderstandings and the additional complications that may stem from them. It is easy to misinterpret an explanation. The customer could be defining the problem one way and you could be processing it another way. Imagine how difficult it would be to arrive at an equitable solution when you are not even talking about the same thing to begin with. Make sure the customer is familiar with the terms you use so he knows exactly what you mean. Define terms clearly. The more complicated the language, the harder it is to understand, causing people to become discouraged and lose interest or to reject outright the proposed solution.

If a language barrier prevents you from reaching an agreement, find a way to overcome the barrier. Is there someone else who can interpret for the customer or is there another way to get your point across to him? Could you write the information, giving the customer additional time to process the words? Always be sensitive to cultural differences. In addition, be aware of generational differences that might hinder progress toward a solution. Keep an open mind.

A debate could cause unnecessary conflict. Never buy into negative behavior or raise your voice to outdo the customer. Try to read the customer's mood to determine the best way to defuse tension and find common ground. If you can determine his temperament, you might figure out the best way to communicate with him.

Project your desire and eagerness to provide excellent customer service by being helpful and flexible. Identify the benefits the customer will receive if he accepts your proposed solution. People are generally interested in what is in it for them when a recommendation is made. Involve the customer in the decision-making process to the extent you can. Keep asking questions and double-check to make sure the customer understands what you are proposing and is satisfied with the solution you have offered.

Brainstorm ideas to work out another solution if the customer is not satisfied with your proposal. Repeat this procedure until a solution has been reached or until you have exhausted all probability of reaching an equitable agreement. When you send the customer on his way happy and satisfied, he will probably return when he needs similar products and services. He might also pass along his positive enthusiasm for your company to his friends.

Not everyone will be satisfied with the solutions offered to them. There may be no way for you to reach an equitable agreement on behalf of both parties. Rather than force an unpopular decision on a customer, you may need to consult with higher-ups or otherwise compromise on your end or the customer's. Take a look at how others in the industry resolve similar problems. Would their techniques work for your company?

Your company may not be at fault for the customer's problem. Even when the customer is wrong, never blame him for causing the problem or accuse him of wrongdoing. You will prevent a more serious problem, as customers do not want to be told they are wrong. They want the problem fixed. Explain your company's position and the reasons why you cannot give the customer what he wants. Be clear about the facts behind your decision. Maintain a helpful, friendly attitude. Concentrate on retaining the customer's business for the long term.

Keep a positive attitude when problems arise. Be polite even when a customer is rude, but do not put up with abusive behavior or allow the customer to bully you. Do not shout at a customer or hurl insults at him. You also do not want to grant the customer something that will cause your company to lose a lot of time or money.

Find the solution that works best for everyone involved. Be fair to the customer.

4.

Strive to Provide Quality Products and Service

One of the primary ways to avoid customer complaints and service problems is to provide quality products and services to every customer every time. Set a high standard of quality for yourself and your company and strive to attain it every day. This initial attention to excellence will pay for itself many times over in customer satisfaction, saving the company time and money.

When you provide high-quality products and/or services, it becomes easy to provide excellent customer service because customers will most likely be highly pleased. Customers who feel they are getting the best possible products and service may be inclined to not overreact to a problem if it develops and will give you their repeat business. On the other hand, if a customer feels products are inferior or service is shoddy, he will be more apt to complain strongly or to find other faults with that product and the company that provided it. He is likely to spread the word among his friends that your company provides terrible products and services and does not care about its customers.

You will save yourself time, money, and headaches by ensuring the quality of everything you provide is to the highest standards. Focus on quality throughout the entire process of developing products and providing service. Accept your share of responsibility for making sure products are flawless. If you are providing a service, make sure the job is done right the first time. If you are in a supervisory position, hold your subordinates accountable for providing consistent, high-quality work.

Be proactive by always keeping the lines of communication open to be sure you and the customer understand each other with regard to quality and service. Find out what the customer's expectations are so you are sure quality means the same thing to both of you. When in doubt, defer to the customer's wishes.

Another key to successful customer service is to really get to know what your customers think about your products and how they use them. By doing so, you can keep customers abreast of upgrades to those products and services and disseminate up-to-date information to them. Ask customers their opinions about all aspects of the products and services you provide them. How do they use your products and services? Are they getting the intended use out of them? What additional products and services can you offer them? Let them know you are always thinking about them. What do your customers think of the quality of your products and services? Do they operate as expected? Do customers feel your products perform to high standards? If they have an unfavorable view, ask for specifics. You can also ask for suggestions. How can you improve? What other products and services would they like to see offered?

By keeping your customers' interests in mind, you will be in an excellent position to provide them with the best possible products for their needs and give them unsurpassed customer service. That, in turn, will keep them coming back.

Develop a customer service survey and solicit feedback. Make it easy for customers to let you know how your company is doing. Customer opinions are invaluable. The feedback you obtain could lead to improvements and new products.

Make quality a priority and provide outstanding products and services.

5.
Be Creative When Solving Customer Problems

Sometimes you need to be creative when solving problems that do not have a simple solution. Broaden your sense of what is possible by thinking outside the box. This method of approaching problems expands the prospects for acceptable solutions. Focusing on possibilities brings more options and opportunities to the table. Use your imagination to the fullest by going beyond the norm and trying a completely new approach. You may be able to deliver far more than you thought possible.

You cannot truly come up with an acceptable solution until you know exactly what the customer wants and what you can do to accommodate that. By knowing what a customer wants, you will be able to address her concerns in a systematic way. Ask the customer what she wants and listen to her answer without placing judgment or forming an opinion until you have all the facts. Missing key components of her complaint may lead to glitches and misunderstandings.

Focus your attention on the customer. Concentrate on what she is saying and remain mentally present throughout the explanation, even if it seems tedious. If necessary, take notes to keep you on track and to compile accurate information. If you are still not sure exactly what the customer wants, restate the problem and her proposed solution as you understand them or ask for clarification of points of which you are uncertain. By understanding your customer's needs, you have the opportunity to satisfy her.

Take care to show the customer you have her interest in mind, not just yours. You do not want to alienate the customer before you have had a chance to address her complaint. Never become defensive or agitated or act bored. You want to gather the facts in an unemotional, unbiased manner.

Although a customer may be critical of you because of your products, try not to get caught up in the drama of what happened. Rather, shift your focus to the solution. Overlook negative comments and blame hurled at you or your company. Emphasize the positive.

After carefully considering the problem and possible options, can you resolve the problem to your and the customer's satisfaction in a timely manner?

In addition to finding a resolution to the customer's complaint, you may also wish to offer her something extra for her trouble and to build goodwill. Even a small gesture could solidify a customer's loyalty.

If you find you or the company are at fault, immediately offer your apologies and express your desire to make amends. If the problem is no fault of yours, you may wish to apologize anyway to maintain goodwill and to get off to a good start toward resolution. Remember, you always want to retain future business if possible.

If you feel the problem is a result of something the customer did and your company cannot be responsible for replacing or fixing the product or service, state the facts in a clear, unemotional manner taking care not to offend the customer. If a customer becomes belligerent or abusive, call a supervisor or otherwise disengage from the incident as quickly as possible.

Address the Problem

Ask yourself questions such as these:

- What is the customer's complaint?
- Is the customer's complaint legitimate?
- What needs to happen to solve this problem and send the customer on her way happy?
- What can I personally do to solve the problem?
- What do I need the customer to do?
- Do I need to involve anyone else in the resolution of this problem?
- What does the solution mean for the customer?
- What does the solution mean for the company?
- How can I ensure future customer satisfaction?
- What can my company do to ensure future customer satisfaction?

Promote the desired benefit of the solution for the customer. She will be more receptive to the solution if she can immediately realize its worth to her.

Work on a Solution

Negotiate a workable solution if possible. Ask the customer questions to determine exactly what she wants you to do about her complaint. Ask questions like the following:

- How do you think we should solve this problem?
- How can we make the situation better for you?
- What would you like us to do?
- What are your suggestions for solving this problem?
- How can we make you happy?
- How would you like the problem handled?
- How would you handle the problem?
- What resolution would be satisfactory to you?

Assess Your Options and Propose a Solution

As with any problem, it is helpful to list your options and analyze them. Try doing the following:

- Ask yourself if you have all the facts about the customer's complaint.
- Determine whether you or the company have encountered this type of complaint before. If so, how was it handled?
- Relate anything else you know about this situation (for example, product performance, customer is a repeat complainer, this person is a faithful customer, etc.).
- Determine whether you need to know anything else about this problem or the options you are considering.
- Think through the situation.
- Choose the best solution of all those you are considering.
- Propose a solution to the customer.
- Take action on the proposed solution.
- Observe the customer's reaction and listen to her response to the proposal.
- Re-analyze the problem if the customer is not receptive to the proposed solution.

Look for solutions outside the ordinary. Dig deep to find unexpected resolutions.

6.
Empathize with the Customer

Have you ever wished someone would just listen to you or try to see things from your side? Your customer may feel the same way when explaining what he needs or when he has a complaint. Put yourself in his place to understand his point of view and gain a better understanding of his problem. Sincerely try to understand, to the extent you can, what the customer is going through. This understanding may result in a swifter resolution of the problem bothering him.

Focus on thinking matters through and proposing options. If you were in the customer's situation, how would you feel? How would you want to be treated? What outcomes would you want to see for the situation?

How would you go about solving the customer's problem? Would you be satisfied with that response if you were the customer? Would you readily accept the proposed solution, given his circumstances?

Always be attentive to your customers. They will be adversely affected by indifference to their situation on the part of any employee. They may even stop doing business with a company if they perceive employees think their complaints or problems are insignificant. Never give customers the impression you do not care about them or what they are going through.

Companies know lost customers may be irreplaceable, so of course they want them to keep coming back. Concentrate on doing your part to promote terrific service and customer satisfaction. Even small actions can have either a negative or a positive impact. If you cannot do what a customer wants, see if there is any step at all you can take to satisfy him.

Realize that your treatment of the customer and his complaint may have widespread implications for his future business and that of everyone he tells about his problem and your proposed solution.

Look for common interests with the customer so you can better connect with him. Your intention should be to promote understanding and to help him.

Ask yourself these questions:

- How can I better understand the customer?
- Have I listened carefully to the customer's explanation of the problem without judgment?
- How can I better see things from the customer's point of view?
- What are some reactions I might expect from this customer?

- How can I keep my reactions professional and positive?
- How can I best help the customer to send him away happy?
- What are the unique challenges this customer faces concerning this problem?
- What are the unique challenges I face in trying to solve this customer's problem?
- How might I solve this problem to the satisfaction of the customer and the company?
- If I cannot solve this customer's problem, is there someone else who can?

Sometimes customers will approach you in an angry, irritated, difficult, or unreasonable frame of mind. Do your best to look past the negative behavior and get to the root of the problem. Show you care about their situation. Hear their complaints with an open mind. Watch for nonverbal clues and words and phrases that indicate important information they are giving to you. Do facial expressions, gestures, or posture indicate the customer is irritated or angry? Are tone and language sarcastic or resentful? Also check for hidden meanings. Let customers know you are in the customer-service business and are committed to helping them receive satisfaction.

Of course, you do not have to subject yourself to abuse from a customer. If a customer gets out of hand, call a supervisor or follow your company's procedures with regard to such situations.

Put yourself in the customer's place. See things from his point of view.

7.

Remain Levelheaded

In an ideal world, we would all let the everyday aggravations and annoying personalities roll off us. However, sometimes it only takes one serious problem or a confrontation with one thorny personality to send us into an emotional tailspin that robs us of time and energy and stresses us out.

Do yourself a favor and cool down before confronting someone who has angered you, or take a step back before dealing with serious problems. Do not give away your power by losing control of your emotions. Your loss of control could be a boost to the other person's position in the matter. Take responsibility for your actions at all times.

Sometimes you have to confront a situation immediately, even when you are angry. In such cases, constantly remind yourself to remain professional and do whatever is required to keep your anger under control.

If there is no way you can avoid a confrontational person—perhaps someone you work with daily—you may want to talk things over with your supervisor or a trusted colleague. Do whatever you can to minimize the stress and aggravation this person causes you. If there is no way you can avoid dealing with a repeat customer who is consistently confrontational, you may want to ask a supervisor or trusted colleague for advice on handling the problem. Some tips to help you keep your cool include taking deep breaths, meditating, repeating affirmations to yourself, and focusing on solutions.

It is especially important to keep your emotions under control at all times when dealing with customers, as they are the backbone of business. This often requires a great deal of patience when confronted with disgruntled, irate, or even belligerent customers who seem to want to take out their frustrations on you. Never let your irritation show. It helps if you remember not to take a customer's anger personally. He is looking for satisfaction for what he believes is a problem.

You never have to put up with abusive behavior from customers, however. Let them know in a professional manner when they are overstepping a boundary. Call on a supervisor if warranted.

Treat everyone with fairness and respect. Take a step back when you feel yourself becoming agitated.

8.

Be Articulate

People are often judged by the way they speak. For instance, a person who uses slang and improper grammar may be judged as illiterate. Someone who uses proper grammar and word choices and who speaks fluently would generally be considered educated. If a person speaks with an accent, he may be perceived to be from a different area of the country or another culture. Of course, these judgments and perceptions may be incorrect.

To avoid negative perceptions, use proper grammar and pronunciation. Say "yes" instead of "yeah" and "no" instead of "nope." Avoid slang expressions such as "ain't" and double negatives like "don't got no." Become familiar with common business terminology.

A professional who speaks well can hold an audience's attention through her use of words and how she expresses them. She is effective whether addressing an audience of one or many. You need not be an expert speaker, but an articulate person has a higher chance of attaining career success.

Realize that words have the power to persuade and influence someone or to fall on deaf ears. What you say and how you say it speaks volumes. Observe your speech habits. Are you easily understood when you speak? Do you notice people paying attention to your every word? A positive answer to these questions means you are on the right course.

Do people tune you out or interrupt you in the middle of your conversations? Do people ask you to repeat what you have said or to speak up? Positive answers to these questions could mean you need to work on your speaking skills. The main question to consider is, does your audience seem confused or are they nodding in understanding? If people do not understand you, communication is lost.

Make it a point to be articulate by using a vocabulary appropriate for your audience, avoiding slang, speaking clearly and slowly, and emphasizing specific key words you want remembered. Speak up loud enough to be heard but not so loud as to annoy or insult someone.

Filter annoying words from your speech—for example, "like," "you know," "yeah," "uh," and similar words. Watch your tone, as how you say something influences your audience as much as what you say. Avoid mumbling or muttering under your breath. Never shout at customers, co-workers, or supervisors.

If a customer is having a difficult time understanding you, think of ways to make it easier for her. For instance, spell the word orally or in writing. When saying hard-to-distinguish letters (e.g., the letters B, C, and E), use a word to identify the letter, such as "B as in 'boy.'"

Associate with articulate people. Observe their use of language and how they interact with others. How can you emulate them to become a better speaker, whether you are addressing one person or several?

Improve your vocabulary through reading. Choose materials appropriate to your situation. Consistently add new words by making a list of words you can study and use to improve your conversations.

Think about the person with whom you are speaking and use language appropriate for that person's background. Pay attention to the person's body language. Does her facial expression indicate an understanding of the message? What do other nonverbal cues say to you?

Speak clearly, use proper diction, and increase your vocabulary.

9.

Greet Customers with a Firm Handshake and Maintain Eye Contact

Remember your manners when dealing with customers. A general rule of etiquette is to be considerate and respectful to everyone. Greet customers in a friendly, welcoming manner. Look him in the eye and ask, "How may I help you?" Use a sincere tone and show genuine interest. People can tell when you are faking.

Shake Hands

Shaking hands is a confusing aspect of greeting people. Should you or should you not shake hands? Who should initiate the handshake? If you do not feel like shaking a hand when one is extended, how do you get out of the situation? If you have sweaty palms and someone wants to shake hands, what should you do?

When it comes to making a good first impression, meeting people, offering thanks, congratulating someone, or otherwise greeting people, the handshake might say as much or more than your words.

Handshaking is not a universal activity. People worldwide do not shake hands in the same way. Professionals must be aware of cultural differences and learn how to greet people properly. A variety of handshaking practices are used in other countries. Learn the handshake practices for co-workers who are from countries other than yours and for repeat customers from other cultures. Be sensitive to the cultural preferences of others.

In the United States, use a firm, confident handshake, but do not grip the customer's hand so tightly as to cause discomfort. If your hands are sweaty, dry them first. A limp, damp handshake is a turnoff. Lean slightly forward, smile, and make eye contact. Offer a brief, suitable greeting. Failure to shake an extended hand in a business situation is often seen as rude and a breach of etiquette. Usually, the higher-ranking individual or the person in charge should make the first move to shake hands. If you are in an individual office, the person to whom the office belongs should initiate the handshake.

Be Welcoming

Use a person's name as soon as it is given and continue to use it throughout the conversation. You might say something like this: "Yes, Mr. Smith, how may I help you?" As the conversation proceeds, look for other ways to use the customer's name such as this: "I will see what I can do, Mr. Smith, and get right back to you on the matter." Using a person's name adds a personal touch to your conversation and conveys that you treat a person as an individual and not just as a problem.

Do not forget to say please and thank you when appropriate. Courtesy leaves others with a favorable impression of you and your company. Avert conflicts by avoiding abrupt, rude conversations.

When given a nametag, wear it on the right. People shake with their right hands. As two people shake hands, their lines of vision may be pulled from the right hand up the arm and to the nametag. This gives both individuals a chance to learn each other's names.

Although you want to maintain eye contact to show you are attentive, avoid staring at someone, which could be construed as bold, domineering, or arrogant. Also avoid behavior that might be thought of as overly friendly. Stay within the bounds of appropriateness and professionalism.

Greet everyone in a welcoming, professional way. Remember your manners.

10.

Be Direct but Diplomatic

The ability to get along with others is one of the most valuable skills in the workplace. One factor that affects this ability is diplomacy, or finding a way to keep the peace. It requires give and take from both parties.

Consider the other person's feelings, background, culture, and understanding of the situation whenever you need to tackle a problem or challenging situation. Her perception may be dramatically different from yours because of her background, culture, and life experiences, necessitating that you clarify points and perhaps compromise.

Sometimes you may have to deliver negative information or a valid criticism of someone's work or behavior. Avoid using absolutes in comments, such as "You used this product improperly," or "You always complain about our service," or "There is nothing I can do to fix this." Be judicious when arriving at conclusions, stating information, and reviewing the details.

Check your delivery and eliminate negative behavior. Do you talk down to your customers? Are you being pushy or bossy when selling to them or when addressing their concerns? Do you demean others or use sarcasm? Do you act like a know-it-all and treat customers as if they do not understand? Ideally, you will be able to answer no to all of these questions.

Be clear and direct, but professional, when you speak to customers. Although you want to be honest and open, you do not want to cross the line and display rude, tactless behavior in your approach. However, do not merely drop hints hoping people will catch on and amend their behavior. They rarely do either.

Always use courtesy and discretion so as not to offend. Be cautious. Do not say exactly what you think if it is inappropriate, hurtful, or untruthful.

When you have important information to deliver, get to the point quickly. Avoid a "how's the weather?" attitude and getting off track, which may confuse the listener and cause your message to be lost or misinterpreted.

Let people know why you are giving information, delivering criticism, or asking them to do something. Discuss your reasons in a positive way, concentrating on what everyone needs to do. Try to inspire people to accept your decision rather than force them. If there is resistance, do not become angry or frustrated. Focus on the benefits of accepting the decision and the benefits of carrying out the decision.

Be straightforward, but use tact and discretion.

2

DEVELOP A WORK ETHIC

Supervisors expect employees to come to the job with a good work ethic. This includes supporting the supervisor, getting along with co-workers, showing up every day and on time, doing the job in an efficient manner, and keeping personal business out of the workplace. Employees must follow policies and procedures if their company is to prosper.

Employees who have a high energy level and are motivated in all aspects of their work are valued for their efficiency and timeliness. Use the steps in this chapter to develop the self-discipline you will need to do your job in an efficient, timely manner.

11.

Support Your Supervisor

Do you find it easy to get along with your supervisor? Because you will be working closely with your supervisor and taking orders from her, it is imperative to do all you can to have a productive work relationship. By developing a successful relationship, you will bring your boss's goals into alignment with yours. As you gain influence with her, your collaborative effort will make for an environment of mutual trust and respect.

As is the case in dealing with anyone, personalities come into play. You will not be a productive team unless you adapt to your supervisor's personality and work habits. Ways to effectively connect include considering the supervisor's personality and moods and tailoring your timing and style to her habits. If she is serious-minded or seems preoccupied with business, act in a professional, no-nonsense manner. If she is annoyed, angry, or upset, steer clear or lend an ear depending upon the circumstances and her particular preference at that time. If she is upbeat and happy, mirror that mood as well. Make an effort to anticipate and then adjust your schedule according to hers. This simple technique will get you on the same page as the supervisor and make it easier for her to communicate how you can assist her. Good communication enhances any work relationship.

Know your supervisor's mission for the company and take steps to help her carry out that mission. Identify what is important to her and support the goals she is attempting to achieve by doing your part to meet them. Give your boss the support she needs to perform her job effectively. When your supervisor succeeds at attaining her goals, everybody who works for the company wins. Make helping her a priority. Sometimes supporting the supervisor can be as simple as listening to the latest workplace problem or contributing ideas as she brainstorms. Think of your support as part of your job.

Ask your supervisor questions similar to these:

- Is there anything I can do for you?
- How can I help?
- Can I take that project off your hands?
- Can I help you finish that project?

Supervisors have differing management styles. One supervisor might be the type who tells employees specifically what to do, making all decisions himself without employee input. He may be the kind who adheres to the rules and expects complete compliance from subordinates. Perhaps he is of the mind to persuade people to do as he wishes rather than ordering subordinates. He may even invite subordinates to contribute to the decision-making process.

You can see how these various supervisors' personalities could influence how subordinates act and react. You may want to research managerial styles to determine how best to mesh with your supervisor's style. In addition to management styles, you will want to consider personality and work habits.

You may have a supervisor whose personality clashes with yours and adversely affects your performance and job satisfaction. She is unlikely to change, so you will need to become more tolerant of her behavior. If you cannot adapt, you might think about moving on to a new job rather than developing a negative attitude and being miserable every day.

To help determine your supervisor's style, ask questions such as these:

- Does my supervisor explain his directives?
- Does my supervisor consult with me when making decisions?
- Does my supervisor keep me informed about policies and directives?
- Does my supervisor assign tasks to me without my input?
- Does my supervisor welcome my ideas?
- Does my supervisor expect complete compliance to company procedures or is he lenient?
- Does my supervisor procrastinate?
- What does my supervisor expect from me?
- Is my supervisor a competent leader?
- Does my supervisor want my help with his tasks?

Knowing your boss's personality and work habits allows you to adjust your own attitude and habits to accommodate and complement his.

Show the supervisor you are behind him and his goals and are not just out for your own agenda. Let him know you are willing to do more than just get by; you are committed to the company and your job. Show him you are passionate about making positive contributions and that you understand how those contributions fit into the big picture.

There may be times when you will have to take criticism from a supervisor. Sift through the criticism to learn what must be corrected to gain the supervisor's approval. If you find yourself being victimized by a bad boss, you should consider finding another job. Of course, if he crosses legal lines, you could turn to the appropriate agency for assistance.

Support your supervisor's goals. Learn to relate to her.

12.

Be Energetic

Effective employees who stand out at work display a high level of energy that drives them to complete tasks with enthusiasm and passion. They are often leaders, but even when they are not, they share leadership qualities such as a high degree of energy. Most have stamina and a never-give-up attitude along with the ability to find ways to increase their energy if it fades.

To show you are an energetic person, give 100 percent effort on every task. If you find yourself not giving 100 percent on important tasks and projects, ask yourself if you are the right person for the job. If you are not committed to doing the job, change your outlook and do your best or perhaps seek support from co-workers who can help boost your enthusiasm. If possible, do not take on projects for which you are not totally committed.

If you seem to have less energy than your co-workers or the average person in your position, try to figure out why. You may need to schedule a medical checkup or a session with a health professional to be sure your low energy is not due to a health problem. After ruling out physical, mental, or emotional health problems, look for other clues. Do you like the work you do? Is the job challenging enough? Are your co-workers enthusiastic? Is your environment safe and pleasant? Are you taking care of yourself?

Increase your lagging enthusiasm by giving yourself pep talks. Telling yourself and your co-workers that you are tired is no way to perk yourself up; rather, you will remain fatigued and likely be further drained of energy. When you feel yourself dragging, talk yourself into acting energetic rather than moping around complaining about how tired you are.

Avoid complacency. Often, boredom, stagnation, and repetitive routine work deplete energy levels. If you suspect these culprits are stealing your energy, look for ways to vary your routine. Ask your supervisor to give you more meaningful tasks. Having important, satisfying work is energizing.

Another way to vary your routine is to find fulfilling interests outside of work that give you the ability to create balance in your life. Balance creates a well-rounded person, which in turn will add to overall effectiveness.

Associate with high-energy co-workers and let their enthusiasm boost you. Complainers, whiners, and sulkers are enough to drain anyone's energy. Attitudes are contagious. Connect with people who spread positivity.

It is difficult to maintain energy levels if you don't have enough rest or you eat too much of the wrong foods. Be sure to get enough sleep and eat healthy foods. Learn to relax even at work. Practice breathing techniques, take mind breaks, meditate while on your lunch break, and so on. Drink alcohol only in moderation.

The right exercise program might be another way to boost energy levels. If you do not have time for a lengthy exercise routine, try doing short bursts of exercise a few minutes at a time several times a day. At work you might go for a walk during break times to shake off drowsiness or to give yourself a change of scenery.

Stress is a big energy stealer. Take care of your health and take preventative measures to keep stress levels low and energy high. Realize that stress is based on your perception, and you can always change your perception. Is there another way to look at a situation? Will that viewpoint lower your stress level? If so, adopt it. Gaining control of your life and your view of things may lessen your stress. When situations seem out of control, concentrate on what you can change.

Most people have high- and low-energy periods. Take advantage of your personal energy levels by scheduling important or difficult tasks for your high-energy time periods and less important tasks for low-energy periods.

Do not let the task of making decisions drain you of energy. Gain control by weighing options and arriving at decisions quickly.

Zap time-wasters. If you suspect that any of the following are wasting valuable time, eliminate or minimize them.

- Disorganization
- Lack of planning
- No goals or inappropriate ones
- Not prioritizing effectively
- Complainers
- Chatty co-workers
- Putting off tasks
- Avoiding decisions

Maintain a level of energy that allows you to complete your work efficiently. Keep yourself in top physical and mental health.

27

13.
Accept Authority

Let's face it: Most people do not like being bossed around. But unless you own the company, you will have a boss. Even bosses have bosses or someone to whom they report. By agreeing to work for an individual or a company, you essentially agree to uphold its policies and procedures. This includes respecting those in authority.

Most employees report to higher-ups. As adults, it is sometimes difficult to defer to another person's directives and instructions. To be successful in your career, you may have to take orders that you are not happy about from higher-ups who are in a position to implement those demands. This becomes even more challenging when reporting to someone who is younger than you or who has different values from you. A supervisor might also operate with a management style you do not like or with an attitude for which you do not care.

Try to relate to the supervisor. Realize his position may be a lonely one. It is hard to be friends with employees when you are the boss. He will not want to appear to show favoritism by being too friendly or by taking part in personal activities with employees. He is also the one who will shoulder the blame when decisions go wrong or when the work is not completed to satisfaction. He must make tough decisions that affect his subordinates.

Of course, you will not want to follow orders that are illegal or that harass, intimidate, or discriminate against you or anyone else.

In today's workplace, several generations often work together and younger supervisors often oversee older workers. If you are in the position of being an older worker reporting to a younger boss, keep the situation in perspective. Perhaps he has the necessary educational or technical skills that you lack. Maybe there is a better way of doing things than what you have done in the past and he can teach it to you. Let go of the attitude that you are more qualified than a younger person. You may be an expert, but rather than present a condescending attitude, why not be open-minded? Can you learn something from him? Could he be a mentor in his areas of expertise? Can you be a mentor to him?

Here are tips for dealing with a younger supervisor if you are an older worker:

- Acknowledge that he may have better technological skills than you.
- Be open to learning new skills from him; ask for feedback.
- Realize he may want to bring changes. Be open to change and acknowledge that the old ways of doing things may be outdated.
- Acknowledge that his way of doing things may be better than the way things have always been done.
- Be a mentor. Help him acclimate and reach his potential.
- Do not demean him or sabotage his efforts.
- Encourage his creativity and independent thinking.

If you are a younger worker who supervises an older worker, remember his value and loyalty to the company. He may be just the expert you need to keep the company running smoothly. His valuable skills could lead to better ways of doing the job. Treat him fairly and professionally. Could the older worker be a mentor to help you learn the ropes and smooth the way with other workers? Can you be a mentor to him?

Here are some tips for dealing with an older worker if you are a younger supervisor:

- Recognize her contributions to the company and her loyalty.
- Be open to learning about how she completed her job in the past. It may still be viable.
- Realize she may not want to change the way she has always done things. Win her over rather than force her to accept your fresh ideas.
- Be a mentor. Offer to help her learn new procedures.
- Provide training to help her learn new technologies and procedures.
- Be sensitive to her needs.
- Acknowledge her prior life experience.
- Be respectful of her and her knowledge of the job.
- See the potential in every employee.
- Be accessible.

When multiple generations work together, some negative attitudes may surface, such as resentfulness, nervousness, arrogance, and the like. On the other hand, positive attitudes may prevail, such as kindness, helpfulness, and cooperation. All generations can learn from one another.

Here are tips for generations of all ages working together:

- Acknowledge that others may have diverse learning styles, habits, and character traits.
- Keep an open mind.
- Keep the lines of communication open.
- Do not take criticism personally. Learn from it.
- Leave your comfort zone and find ways to relate to each other.
- Handle your job in a professional, respectful manner.
- Be respectful of others' positions.
- Never become arrogant or a know-it-all.

You have a right to be treated fairly in the workplace. Continual criticism, put-downs, negativity, and conflicts involving a supervisor can lead to stress and low self-esteem. When a supervisor is unfair and makes your work life miserable, you may want to consider a different position. The company may decide to keep the supervisor and not interfere with how he treats employees as long as he is operating within the parameters of the law. This means he may be free to use criticism and negativity in handling subordinates.

If you feel you are being wrongfully treated, schedule a meeting with the supervisor and ask him what you have done to warrant such treatment. If you are at fault, find out how you can best remedy the situation. If you are not at fault and do not receive satisfaction from meeting with the supervisor, follow your company's chain of command in reporting the incident.

Make it a point to get along with people in authority. Be open-minded.

14.
Be Self-Motivated

One of the greatest challenges to completing a goal is being motivated to stick with it. This is true whether the goal is a simple task, a complex project, or a lifetime commitment.

It is one thing to begin a task, but it is another to motivate yourself to keep going until the task is finished. How many times have you started something and then abandoned it before you finished? Motivation is key to seeing something through, but it is not always easy to be self-motivated. One thing that can help you stay on task is to figure out what might motivate you to keep moving forward. What is the reason behind what you do? Your reasoning could be positive or negative. Going to work every day so you will not be fired would be a motivator, albeit a negative one. Saving money to buy your dream house would be a positive motivator.

When you truly want to do something and are passionate about it, motivation comes easy. Doing something you do not like to do is not motivating. You will need to find a compelling enough reason to keep going. Is that possible? What are the benefits of completing the task? You will find it easier to motivate yourself if you enjoy what you are doing and get excited about the task. Can you muster enough excitement to see it through?

For those times you do not feel like doing your job, tell yourself that once you get started, a weight will be lifted. Is there one thing you can do to get started? Small steps whittle away at big projects. After you get into the workflow, you may even begin to look forward to completing the project.

Be passionate about your work. Find meaning in all you do. Focusing on a passion is a strong motivator. When you truly believe in your work, you are willing to devote the necessary time and energy to it.

Self-motivated people push themselves to complete what they start even when the excitement wears off. When your motivation lags, put pressure on yourself to find a way to push yourself. Sometimes it takes sheer willpower to pick up the pen, take another step, read one more page, put another part together, or do whatever you must to keep going, but make the commitment. Remember, if you quit, you will never finish. Chart your progress and build on each of your successes, even small ones. The main thing is to keep going.

Feed your mind positive, motivational information. There are hundreds of self-improvement books, CDs, and videos that present any number of ways to boost morale and motivate people, including you. Friends, family, co-workers, and other people can inspire you. Spend time with individuals who inspire you.

Avoid taking a wait-and-see attitude about your work. Do something. Just start. Keep going and don't stop until you are finished. If you must interrupt your momentum, make sure it is for a valid reason. Get back on task as quickly as possible.

If you have a problem to solve, address it immediately. Do not think about how difficult it is; accept the challenge. Brainstorm ideas and make a list of possible solutions along with the pros and cons. Come up with the best solution and put it into play. Create a vision of the successful outcome you hope for and keep it in the front of your mind.

What excuses are holding you back? No time? Limited skills? Poor equipment? You do not know how to approach the problem at hand? No cooperation from team members? The list could go on and on. These and other excuses may cause you to drift aimlessly instead of focusing attention where it needs to be. Your excuses may be valid, but look beyond them.

What can you gain control over? If you do something about those areas of your life you are making excuses for, you have the possibility of eliminating those excuses. Take each excuse apart and determine how you can overcome it. Practice time management, upgrade your skills, rent new equipment, and do whatever else you need to do to eliminate an excuse.

Now and then, people deliberately put things off that they know they should do. This delay turns into procrastination when it develops into a continual pattern of avoiding tasks that must be completed by specific deadlines. People procrastinate for a variety of reasons, including not knowing how to do the task, not wanting to do it, being too introverted to perform the task, being easily distracted, and so on.

To combat procrastination, assess why you procrastinate and develop strategies to break the cycle. Ask yourself the following questions:

- What kinds of tasks do I usually put off doing?
- Why do I procrastinate on those particular tasks?
- What have I put off doing that needs to be done right now?
- Why am I putting off this particular task?
- What am I gaining by not doing this task?
- Can I do something about the reason I am putting off this task?
- What will happen if I do not do this task?
- Will others be affected if I do not do this task?
- What would make me take action on this task?
- What one step right now could I take toward completing this task?
- What prevents me from taking that one step?

- Can anyone else help me do this task?
- How will I feel when this task is completed?

Create a daily to-do list and set priorities. Schedule work so important tasks are first on the list, ensuring deadlines are met. Put excuses and procrastination behind you once and for all and commit to doing whatever you need to do to take care of business. Focus on starting, not finishing, the project. Break it down into step-by-step tasks. Begin. Making excuses will not get the job done. Focus on the rewards of finishing a job. Hold yourself accountable by telling co-workers and supervisors what you will accomplish. The fear of letting everyone down may be enough to push you to finish.

Become a leader, not a follower. Adopt a proactive mindset that will allow you to always be in the forefront of decisions and solutions. Offer suggestions you think will benefit you and the company. If your suggestions are rejected, do not take it personally or let that keep you from making other suggestions you think would be beneficial. Sometimes ideas are not feasible for a particular time and situation.

If you do find that a problem or task stresses or overwhelms you, take a break, but have a plan in place to pick up where you left off in a timely manner. No matter what goes wrong, a positive change or outcome is possible. A negative outlook is detrimental to finding a positive outcome. Remain optimistic.

Sometimes just thinking about what you have to do wears you down. Instead, focus on something positive. Have you completed any part of the job? Can you do something now? How good will you feel when the job is completed? Will others be positively affected when you finish? What will the finished project look like?

If you are going to talk to yourself, make it encouraging. Stop telling yourself a task is too difficult or you do not like to do it or you will never get it done. People overcome significant challenges every day to become the best at what they do.

What happens if you make a mistake or somehow derail the project? How do you counter such disappointment in yourself and from others? Understand your limits in reaching any decision. Things often go wrong for no apparent reason. Keep the benefits of finishing the job foremost in your thoughts. It is better to have tried than not to have tackled the problem at all. Admit the mistake; do not make excuses. Offer to fix the problem. Revise your plan and try something else. Work on rebuilding your self-esteem. Remind yourself that the low periods will pass. Ask for help when you are overwhelmed or inundated with work. Recall your successes.

Do something. Take a step and another until you have completed the task.

15.
Be Self-Disciplined

Why is it some people finish tasks in record time while others barely get anything accomplished? Why do some people manage their time and stay organized while others do not, even though they know they should? Why do some people jump right in while others procrastinate, dally, or do nothing?

It takes self-discipline to start and to finish tasks, manage time, stay organized, take the initiative, and do the work required. It takes discipline to continue doing these things day after day while keeping your mind on the goal. Without discipline, little or nothing is accomplished.

You know what you have to do to get the job done. When you want to accomplish a task, you have to discipline yourself to do it and keep doing it until it is completed. You might not always have the determination to tackle jobs that come your way, but if you do not discipline yourself to forge ahead, you will fall behind. Write and prioritize your to-do list and work your way through it by sheer willpower.

If you have trouble being disciplined, ask yourself why you have not taken action. Are you clear about what it is you are to do? If not, how can you find that clarity? Having a clear understanding of what you need to do is a major contributor to having the discipline to start and then finish a job. Write down what you need to complete the job and meet the deadline. Using daily planning lists and project boards, set reasonable timelines. Begin the task, working in short spurts. Focusing on the task for a few minutes of total concentration is better than spending an hour of unfocused time that accomplishes very little. Short sprints of time may lead you to settle into a rhythm where you can focus for longer periods of time.

Are you dreading a task you do not like? If so, do you really need to do it? Does the task have to be done to perfection or can you do it sufficiently? Will the idea of having a reward to look forward to at the completion of the task spur you to action?

Look for something positive about the tasks you must finish. If you cannot find anything positive about performing the task, perhaps thinking about how wonderful it will feel to finish the task will motivate you. What do you need to do to get started? Can you take that step? If not, why not?

Can you delegate the task to someone else? If so, hand it off to a team member. If you must have a hand in the task, can someone else help you do what you have been putting off? If that is a possibility, ask the person for assistance. If that person cannot help with the task, can she offer some suggestions to help you complete it? Often, having someone as a sounding board is beneficial in gaining the knowledge needed to complete a task or the motivation to begin and keep working.

Make a conscious effort to stop stalling by finding a compelling enough reason to do what you need to do. By doing so, you will be more likely to find the willpower to do something—anything. Get excited about starting and finishing a task, project, or whatever else you need to do. If nothing else, remind yourself how good it will feel to be finished with it.

To take the pressure off yourself, concentrate on small, steady steps. Do one part of the job and congratulate yourself on that achievement, knowing that step brought you closer to the finish line. However, you will not want to drag out the job indefinitely. Commit to completing the task in a reasonable time period by breaking tasks into steps that can be completed by mini deadlines. For instance, if you have a report due, brainstorm ideas one day, write an outline the next, start paragraphs the following day, and so forth. If you can get something started, it is easier to keep up the momentum. Take action every day; stay involved. Do as much as you can each day to reach your desired outcome.

Do you wait until the last possible minute to complete tasks? Ask yourself why. Waiting until the last minute, especially on a big project, means you may be setting yourself up for a high-pressure time crunch that could leave you highly stressed, making mistakes due to haste, and failing to complete the work.

Urge yourself not to wait until the last minute. You can train yourself to create a new habit of starting a project as soon as it is given to you. Establish a workable timeline and do your best to stick to it. Create a sense of urgency that will get you moving in the right direction, but do not cause undue stress for yourself.

Once you begin to apply yourself to the task, you stand a much better chance of continuing. Set reasonable deadlines for yourself and acknowledge your progress each step of the way. Setting your own deadline that occurs before the actual project deadline will allow you to finish the task with time to spare.

Develop a successful routine by scheduling repetitive tasks for regular times when you are least busy, which allows for interruptions. Change up your routine so as not to get bored. Boredom may break down your efforts at self-discipline. If possible, schedule blocks of time for large projects and break them down into manageable chunks. Eliminate as many distractions as you can so you can focus on your obligation.

A self-disciplined person will consistently work toward the desired end result, no matter how long it takes. He knows it is the desired result that matters. Consistent, focused action produces results.

When you find yourself making excuses that disrupt your work, write them down. Find a way to eradicate the excuses.

Carry self-discipline over into all areas of your work life. Maintain an excellent attendance record and be punctual. Prepare for the next day's work before you leave at the end of each day. Stay organized. If you must stop in the middle of a project at the end of the day, jot down a quick note about what comes next so you can easily resume the task the following day.

Eliminate excuses. Do your job. Improve yourself.

16.

Accept Constructive Criticism as an Opportunity for Growth

Most people gladly accept positive feedback on their work, but they are not receptive to criticism. Who likes to be criticized? The first instinct is to protect yourself from the criticism by denying fault, making excuses, blaming others, or feeling hurt. The fact is, however, people make mistakes, and those mistakes must be corrected. One of the problems with criticism is that sometimes people are corrected in a disparaging way that causes them to reject the censure and the person delivering it.

Because mistakes happen and things go wrong, you need to be able to take criticism. Depending on the circumstances, you will have to develop a sense of whether you should respond or keep quiet while being criticized. Sometimes responding to criticism makes the situation worse. You find you are digging yourself into a deeper hole. Even if you feel it is unwarranted, you may be better off at the time to rise above the criticism and remain silent. After you have taken the time to calm down and process the criticism, you may have a different point of view. If you still feel the criticism was unfair, you will be in a better emotional frame of mind to address the issue.

If you are being criticized in front of other people, you may want to delay your response and wait to speak privately to the person who corrected you. Behaving in the same manner as the criticizer will not remedy the situation. It is likely to worsen it. Do not let criticism upset you to the point that you lose your sense of professionalism. Strong emotional reactions do not solve anything. They leave you drained of energy and reflect poorly on your attitude and performance. Take a deep breath.

When you are criticized, try not to take it personally. This may be difficult, but to thrive in your career, it is best to put aside negative feelings and look for an opportunity to grow from the reproach. Sort out key information that will help you become a better employee.

Ask questions if you do not understand where the criticism is coming from or why. If you do not receive a satisfactory answer, ask additional questions until you do but avoid becoming belligerent or hostile. Consider yourself on a fact-finding mission.

Quickly correct problems for which you have been criticized, taking care to be accurate and efficient. Show your adaptability and demonstrate improved performance. Ask to be re-evaluated and seek additional feedback. Establish a reputation as someone who is willing to correct mistakes and to learn from them.

If the person delivering the message or the way in which it was delivered bothers you, look past the delivery method. Pick out the words that will give you the impartial facts. The bottom line is to correct the problem and move forward.

After sorting the facts from the disapproval, if you feel the assessment was unfair or incorrect, inform the person who criticized you. Instead of offering excuses, state the reason why you are not at fault as accurately as possible. Stick to the facts. Allow the other person to respond. If necessary, repeat your position and the facts.

If you continue to be upset by the way in which the message was delivered, seek another opinion. Ask an impartial third party to evaluate the mistake and the ensuing criticism. Talking things over with someone else may help you see something you missed when you sorted the facts from the message and the manner in which it was delivered.

Remember, not everyone is tactful and skilled in conveying censure. That does not mean you should ignore the problem that caused you to be criticized. Ask yourself what the problem is that needs to be addressed. Concentrate on how you can resolve that problem.

When things go wrong, you may have to shoulder the responsibility on behalf of your boss and co-workers or the company. As part of a team, you might have to accept the blame on their behalf.

If you are being criticized by a customer, try not to take it personally. Quite likely, she is annoyed with the company's products or services and is generalizing to include you. If you are the reason for the customer's irritation, find ways to improve the situation.

Sort through criticism to find and resolve the problem. Think of the criticism as an opportunity to learn a lesson.

17.

Be Adaptable

As a rule, people do not like change or dealing with situations out of the norm of how they operate. Unfortunately for them, change is inevitable—and so is managing it.

Situations change at a moment's notice. Anyone who wants to succeed needs to adapt to change in a positive way. There will be times at work when you will need to adapt to your environment, your co-workers and supervisors, and your duties.

If you have been in the same position for a number of years, you may have become complacent. Check to see if your attitude is holding you back or affecting your work or work relationships in any way. If so, make an appropriate attitude adjustment. It is easy to get into a rut and assume the way you have always done things is the best way to do them. If you have always completed things a certain way, and a change in that procedure is suggested or mandated, change your mindset from one of "That is the way I do things" to "I'll give it a try." Make it a practice to question whether a job could be done more efficiently and if so, how.

When co-workers need help with projects, your schedule changes because of a new priority, or you are reassigned tasks or positions, be flexible and adjust to the new situation or schedule. In downsized workplaces, employees must often take on additional tasks and responsibilities without complaining, "That's not my job." These days, everyone pitches in to do what needs to be done.

Interruptions are inevitable in the workplace, requiring you to be flexible with your time. If you expect to be interrupted while working on a project, find ways to minimize those interruptions. Perhaps you could break the task into small enough parts that you will not lose total focus if you have to stop intermittently. Inform co-workers that you are working on an important project that requires total concentration. Could you hang a "do not disturb" sign on your door? Is there a way to arrange to have the interruptions at a convenient time? For instance, if you have a meeting, could you schedule it for first thing in the morning before you begin your tasks?

Embrace technology. It is here to stay. Those who do not accept or adopt it will be left behind. Technology has brought and will continue to bring change to the way tasks are assigned and completed. Technology itself is ever-evolving. What is the optimal way of doing things today might be obsolete tomorrow.

New software, programs, and equipment become available almost daily. We are living in an age where upgrades and new products are a constant; there is no avoiding them. Those who do not adapt will be left behind or let go from the company. Your value to the company decreases markedly when you are unwilling to take on the challenges technology delivers.

You may be called on to take a business trip, attend unscheduled meetings, work overtime or more flexible hours, or deal with any number of requests to keep work moving along and the business running smoothly. Accept these and other changes.

To determine if you are open to change, ask yourself the following:

- Am I willing to embrace new technology?
- Do I keep up with the changes to the technology I use to perform my duties?
- How can I keep up with technological changes in my field?
- Am I willing to deviate from my normal work schedule as needed?
- Do I meet challenges head on?
- Do I willingly help others when called upon to do so?
- Am I flexible in my thinking and in my performance?
- Do I continuously evaluate my performance and my skills?
- Am I open to new ways of doing things?
- Do I have an attitude of change?

Be open to change, and change direction when necessary.

18.
Do Not Complain About Workload

Nowadays, a lot of people could complain about being overworked. Many companies have learned to make do with a leaner workforce, and employees are called on to perform tasks outside their job descriptions. Even job descriptions have blurred lines, meaning employees are asked to do whatever is necessary to get the job done.

When you complain about being swamped with work or not having enough time to complete your work, you run the risk of being seen as having a victim mentality or someone who cannot manage her time. No one wants to hear about your backlog or how much work you do compared to everyone else. When you start comparing yourself to others, you set up a no-win situation. How would you feel if someone told you he did more work than you? How would you feel if you were told you could not possibly be as busy as someone else? That is how people feel when you complain you are doing all the work.

If you do have a complaint or you actually are doing all the work, find a way to broach the subject while offering a reasonable, workable solution. Otherwise, you will be perceived as a complainer. Another way of looking at the work you do is that you are learning valuable organizational skills along with taking on additional responsibility. These aspects may be beneficial the next time you are up for a raise or a promotion.

If you feel you are overworked, complaining solves nothing. The better plan would be to manage your time and prioritize your tasks, and ask for help when absolutely necessary. Complainers spread negativity and discontent throughout the workplace. Employers look for ways to cut negativity.

Chances are if you are so busy, other people are under pressure, too. The boss is probably more interested in what he needs and how to meet productivity goals than in your complaints. Therefore, you will have to be smart in how you handle the situation. If you truly do not have enough hours in the day to complete everything that needs to be done, discuss your situation with the supervisor in a professional manner. Ask for his help or suggestions. Rather than complain, suggest how to remedy the situation by proposing viable solutions. It will help if you walk into the meeting with an idea of how you spend your day. Take your filled calendar and a list of your duties along with an approximate time for completing them. Tell your supervisor what you have done for him and the company and offer suggestions for improving the bottom line.

Commit to what you can deliver and make viable suggestions for clearing your backlog. When reminded of what you promised to do for someone, avoid telling him you have been too busy to complete the work. It conveys you have placed a low priority on his request or he is not a priority for you.

Complete your work without complaint. When you do have a complaint, offer a solution.

19.
Do Not Conduct Personal Business in the Workplace

When you are hired to work for a company, you are expected to complete the company's agenda, not your own personal one. In other words, unless the company sanctions your doing personal work on its time and/or with its equipment, limit personal business in the workplace. This includes, but is not limited to, making phone calls and copies, paying bills, playing online games, and accessing social media. Conducting personal business during company time is a conflict of interest. You are paid by the company for the time you are hired to work for it.

Employees have been known to make personal copies—sometimes hundreds—for parties, organizations they belong to, and so on. They often spend hours per week on the phone or computer doing personal tasks or socializing, which causes companies to place restrictions on their phones and computers to lock employees out of certain locations and also track their movements on the equipment. Other employees read novels or attend to personal grooming like polishing their nails. Unfortunately, employees have even been known to run a personal side business out of their full-time workplaces, using the company phone, fax, and copier for personal business gain. Their personal side business costs the company in time, supplies, and wear-and-tear on equipment, and all the while they are being paid by an unsuspecting employer. It is easy to see how wrong these actions are.

Keep in mind that anything you do with company equipment on company time belongs to the company, not you personally. Avoid using company equipment for personal use, including telephones, fax machines, copiers, and the Internet. The paper, ink or toner, wear-and-tear on equipment, and time used for personal business is very costly to the company.

It is never a good idea to divulge highly personal information to co-workers. Your co-worker may take sides or feel uncomfortable discussing the information. You also run the risk of having her tell others about your business. Alternatively, you may later feel embarrassed or regret that you said anything.

In the event it is necessary for you to conduct personal business during work hours, use common sense and check with your company policy. Many companies are fine with an employee making a brief personal call or taking an emergency call. When the call is to a long-distance number, the company will be charged. Follow set procedures to reimburse the company. If you want to make several personal copies, check with your company's policy or ask your supervisor. If you need to check something on the Internet such as a phone number, follow company Internet policies.

Remember, even if you conduct your personal business on your lunch hour, the equipment and supplies you use belong to the company and may cost the company extra money.

Many employees try to justify helping themselves to company supplies—pens, tape, paper clips, paper, and so on. They take any number and type of supplies home. Office supplies are not job perks or a fringe benefit of working for a company. Supplies are not free; the company pays for them to conduct company business.

Avoid doing personal business on company time.

3

Maximize Your Professionalism

Professionals display a set of common personal traits including loyalty, persistence, accuracy, and charisma. These employees show their versatility in their job performance and their goals. They are willing to take measured risks when necessary and are open to learning all they can about themselves, others, and their jobs.

Professionals work with an eye toward the future. They envision more efficient ways of doing their jobs and perform at their best at all times.

20.
Be Loyal

Loyal employees who are high performers take pride in their work and value their contributions to their employers. They are likely to improve their competency in a number of areas, including skills, leadership qualities, human relations, professionalism, customer service, and more. This strong job commitment tells co-workers and supervisors they believe their work is making a difference to the whole of the organization, and they see the bigger picture and where they fit.

Loyalty carries with it a number of positive characteristics. Loyal employees are more optimistic and extend that attitude to others around them, which makes for pleasing working conditions. Of course, working in a pleasant environment will make your job easier and contribute to camaraderie among your peers.

Employees who are loyal commit fully to a job and undertake it with enthusiasm, which adds to their sense of worth and fulfillment. Their job satisfaction carries over positively in their interactions with customers, co-workers, and managers.

A strong sense of loyalty affects those around you. By displaying loyalty, you demonstrate to co-workers and supervisors that they can trust you to be an engaged, productive member of the team. Your loyalty conveys that you will not let them down and understand your contributions affect more than just you. It says you will work hard for the common cause.

Displaying loyalty will encourage a positive relationship with supervisors, who want employees they can count on and who enjoy working for the company and promoting its policies. If your supervisor makes a decision with which you do not agree, put aside your opinions and stand behind him. Always look at the big picture and not just your feelings.

Align your goals with those of your organization so you avoid becoming someone who merely shows up every day to collect a paycheck. Such an attitude will undermine your self-worth and job contentment. Take pride in giving outstanding effort, which will keep your skills sharp and prove your worth to others.

Another facet of loyalty is to promote your company and co-workers by presenting a united front to the public. Always speak favorably about your company and its mission, your co-workers, and your customers.

Some people question why they should be loyal if their company is not loyal to them. One way to look at it is this: Making an investment in an organization affords an employee the opportunity to learn the industry and to increase personal skills. By committing to help your company prosper and growing along with it, you succeed, even if it means relocating to another organization at a later time.

Customers show their loyalty by coming back to your company and even spreading the word among their friends. Show your loyalty to them by providing what they need along with excellent customer service.

Although you want to be loyal to your company, co-workers, customers, and supervisors, maintain your personal integrity and always seek to do the right thing. You should not be loyal to the extent that you do something illegal or immoral or against your personal code of ethics.

If you find you cannot be loyal to your organization or employer for whatever reason, you may want to consider finding another job where you can express your loyalty.

Develop a strong sense of loyalty and be a person your supervisor, customers, and co-workers can count on.

21.

Be a Visionary

Visionaries operate with the big picture in mind. They consider what will benefit the company as a whole and envision how everything and everyone involved can work together to create the whole company dynamics. They make projections based on the future needs of their organizations. Visionaries are dreamers, but realistic in what they see as a winning situation for themselves and their companies. Visionaries are imaginative; they can imagine things that others do not see or understand. They are always looking for a novel direction, a different method, and fresh prospects.

A visionary does not have crystallized thinking; rather, he is open to changing his thinking as often as necessary for the betterment of himself and the company for which he works. He is open-minded and will listen to the ideas of others. He involves and encourages people around him to participate in the process of creating the company's future.

Forward-thinking people who have an eye on the future ensure that organizations and individuals alike will not become obsolete. Avoid getting stuck in outdated thinking and old habits. Look ahead to what the company and the supervisor might implement. Challenge yourself daily to anticipate future requirements and how to meet them. Develop lists of current business practices and those you would like to see implemented in the future. How can you bring these things to fruition?

Read current information in your field to learn the latest developments, technology, and setbacks so you can be prepared to do your share. Knowing what is on the cutting edge in your field places you in a position to become an expert in an area that will be critical to your company's success and your career with that company. Be attentive to what is happening around you. Question everything—what you observe and your research. How can you use the information you have discovered to improve your productivity? How can you use the information to benefit your company?

Awareness of new developments in the field and within the company will position you to execute them or to devise similar concepts. Will the latest innovations benefit your company? How can you build on those developments? Pay attention to details no matter how trivial they seem. The smallest thing might make a big difference.

Team up with co-workers to share expertise and resources. Talk about current issues. Discuss ways to improve your company's products and services. If you are farsighted, involve co-workers in your overall vision. They may have relevant theories to share.

Surround yourself with visionaries who are inspiring and willing to share their thoughts. Make it a regular practice to get together with them and brainstorm. Select individuals who can identify workable ideas and are not afraid to point out those without merit. Be a person who enjoys meeting with others and exchanging ideas. With an open mind, welcome different viewpoints that may include long-range plans or any number of principles you may not have thought of proposing. Discuss and develop the strongest suggestions presented by the group. List the pros and cons, your co-workers' comments, your research, and the probable paths to implementation. How will implementing the ideas improve job performance or otherwise benefit your company?

Become an idea person by assuming anything is possible and that those possibilities are endless. Do not hold back. Think of everything as an opportunity to do something in a better way by removing limitations you place on yourself. Work around company constraints that might stifle creativity. If you have a difficult time generating ideas, take a break. A worthwhile notion may come to you when you are not focused on coming up with one. Trying too hard may backfire and leave your mind blocked.

When workplace conditions are not conducive to creative thinking, the visionary will create the right conditions. For instance, he might put together a super team of innovative, passionate individuals. Utilizing a team to generate a list of random concepts takes the pressure off you, as no one is singled out to produce that one great idea.

Contribute ideas on saving time and money. Propose ways to complete tasks more efficiently. Offer suggestions on anything you think will improve things for you, the boss, and the company. If your recommendations are not implemented, do not be discouraged. There may be a compelling reason of which you are unaware why the recommendations will not work.

What can you do differently today that will make you more efficient tomorrow or next year or years from now? What can you suggest your company and your co-workers do to become more efficient in the future?

A visionary has the ability to recognize opportunities and take advantage of them. Through passion and energy, he will encourage co-workers and others to join him in these opportunities. Visionaries also have the ability to foresee possible obstacles and challenges, but they do not retreat from them. They know setbacks are part of life. To that end, they also think ahead to anticipate solutions to those obstacles.

To prevent yourself from subconsciously sabotaging your vision for your future and that of your company, set a goal to generate a certain amount of new ideas per week or month. Having the goal could alert your mind to consider ideas even when you are not consciously aware of doing it.

Look at the big picture and how it relates to the future. Keep up with the latest developments in your industry.

22.

Consistently Perform Well

You can be the hardest worker in the company, but if your work is inaccurate, you will be a detriment. Mistakes cost companies time and money. They can also cost a worker his reputation, especially when the mistake is a careless one that should not have happened. Take pride in delivering an outstanding performance every time you do something. Be competent and efficient. Work quickly, but never sacrifice accuracy in your haste to finish a job.

Double-check your work. There is always enough time to do something correctly. It is a waste of time to have to redo work that is incorrect, not to mention that inaccuracies could cost your company in time and money.

Do not go to extremes with your work. Although your goal is accuracy, avoid trying to be a perfectionist. Otherwise, you may never be ready to hand over a project. In addition, your creativity may suffer. Just strive to do your finest work. Developing good judgment and job skills will give you more control over your tasks and responsibilities.

Periodically take note of your strengths and weaknesses so you can make appropriate adjustments. To perform at optimal level, update your skills on a regular basis and keep abreast of the latest information for your field. Your company counts on you to be at the top of your game at all times in all areas of your responsibility. Your work may not be accurate if you have missed an important update in your field or if you do not have the latest skills required to do the work correctly.

By consistently delivering excellent work, you will show others your commitment and your pride in handling your responsibilities. You will develop a reputation as someone who can be counted on to do the job right. People will take you seriously and consult you in areas of your expertise.

If you do make a mistake, admit it, accept responsibility, and take corrective action to right the wrong. Not owning up to your mistakes is a surefire way to undermine your reputation. Repetitive mistakes will take a toll on your credibility. People are apt to be more forgiving when you own up to your shortcomings. Making excuses and blaming circumstances or other people delay the resolution and may create additional problems.

Do your best work at all times. Maintain accuracy and check your work.

23.

Drop the Sense of Entitlement

Often, employees feel the company owes them something more than what they are getting. If you are receiving the pay and benefits the company has promised in return for a certain job you are hired to do for a specified number of hours per day, you are probably receiving everything to which you are entitled. Unless perks are specifically stated, they are usually not part of the hiring agreement.

The company must provide you with a safe working environment, free from discrimination and harassment. If you feel your environment is unsafe, advise the proper personnel. If that does not correct the breach, contact the appropriate agency. If you feel your personal rights are being violated, follow the company policy to bring the violations to the attention of the proper personnel. If you do not feel satisfied with the results, report the matter to the appropriate agency or authorities.

Not receiving the recognition you deserve is a subjective matter. You may feel recognition is deserved, but the supervisor or company may not. Is there a specific policy to cover your situation? Talk to your supervisor to find out what you need to do to ensure you are performing satisfactorily and gaining recognition to which you are entitled. If you feel you have a strong case for having been denied appropriate recognition, discuss the matter with your supervisor in a professional, non-threatening way. Stick to the facts. Do not whine, or complain as you will be perceived as a complainer or troublemaker. If you are not satisfied with the supervisor's answer, you may have to let the matter drop, especially if no laws have been broken.

The office you are in and the equipment and supplies you use belong to the company. Avoid stealing time, information, supplies, merchandise, money, and the like for yourself and others. Rationalizing that the company owes you these things does not make your actions right. Stealing in any form is wrong.

Company policies are meant for everyone and apply to everyone who works for the company. Do not become someone who feels the rules do not apply to him. Take only the allotted time for breaks and lunch. Arrive and leave on time. Do not hide to avoid work or shirk from your tasks. Do your part when you share duties with a co-worker, participate on a team, or must train someone.

In situations where you are working with multiple generations, reject thoughts that you are entitled to special privileges because of your particular age, your length of time with the company, and what or whom you know. If you expect to be treated fairly by everyone, treat everyone fairly.

Be realistic about what the company owes you in return for the services you provide.

24.

Persist

To be successful, keep trying until your reach your goal. Giving up too soon has been the undoing of many people. Who knows if they might have otherwise been successful if they had kept on going? There is a reason people say persistence pays off. It is because without persistence, it would be difficult or even impossible to reach a goal, whether it is completing a simple task or something huge in scope.

Take the time to listen to your thoughts and figure out what you are telling yourself all day long. Replace negative thoughts with positive ones. Positive self-talk is one way to sustain your ability to persist in any situation. Keep reminding yourself of what you will gain if you finish what you set out to do. Tell yourself you can and will do whatever you must do to reach a goal.

The ability to persist is one of the most beneficial character traits you can possess. If you persist over a long enough period of time, you just might find a creative way to solve every problem you encounter and accomplish every goal you set. In many cases it is the constant pushing yourself to perform that brings success—the trying, failing, getting back up, and trying again. This process often leads to inspirations, one of which might work. Often it is one little thing that holds a person back; with persistence, that barrier can be broken.

Commit. People who are 100 percent committed will likely persist until they reach their goal, whether it is finishing a project or learning something new. Do not permit adversity to derail your plans. Everyone encounters difficulties. Desire often gives people a sense of purpose that urges them on when faced with adversity. Find a way to create the kind of desire that will help you bounce back from defeat and disappointment.

You may not be able to change your circumstances, but you always have the choice of trying something else again and again. Think of setbacks as mere learning experiences. If you truly want something, you will be driven to persevere until it comes to fruition. People often persist for years before reaching a goal.

When facing adversity, ask yourself these questions:

- Why did you not succeed?
- What are the barriers between you and what you hope to attain?
- How can you break down those barriers?
- How can you change tactics whenever your effort fails?
- What can you do differently the next time?
- What are some alternative ways for you to attain what you want?

To keep moving forward when you feel like giving up, think about the payoff you will receive when you reach your goal. Keep your eye on your desired outcome. Make up your mind to stick with something for the long term. Do not allow anything to get in the way of your progress.

To keep up your momentum, ask yourself the following questions about your goal:

- Will it be worth the time and effort if you succeed?
- Do you want it enough?
- What will be your reward when you attain what it is that you want?
- Did you put in enough effort?
- Did you put in enough time?
- Are you making the greatest use of your time?
- Do you have the willpower and the stamina to succeed?
- Will it be worth the time and effort if you succeed?
- Would you do something more if you knew you could succeed?
- Could you do something different?

Whenever you must complete a task or reach a specified goal, keep moving forward and persist until you achieve the results you want.

Success depends to a great extent on commitment and persistence.

25.

Develop a Healthy Lifestyle

Healthy people tend to be able to perform their jobs at optimum levels. They generally look at life positively. A healthy lifestyle leads to better physical, mental, and emotional health.

It is difficult to perform at your optimum if you are sick or run down. Unhealthy eating habits, skipping needed rest and sleep, drug and alcohol addictions, and sedentary ways take a toll on the body and mind. These poor habits also take a toll on careers.

Do your best to take care of your health. Everyone knows to get plenty of rest, to exercise regularly, and to eat healthy foods, but doing so is not always easy. If you have difficulty, align with someone who will encourage you or even work with you to develop a healthy lifestyle. It is well worth the effort to maintain your health.

Are you high strung? Find time to relax and de-stress. Clear your schedule; eliminate unnecessary tasks. Find ways to express yourself that do not include yelling, whining, stamping feet, throwing things, or crying. Stress negatively affects health in many ways. If work is a stressor, schedule your most challenging work during your most productive time of the day or night.

Groom yourself every day. Healthy people are attentive to their physical appearance—another trait of professional people who strive to get ahead on the job.

Do your part to help others get healthy. Can you start or else suggest to your supervisor that the company start a stress-management, weight-loss, exercise, or smoking-cessation program in your workplace?

Here are a few more ideas:

- Join a wellness program.
- Join a gym. Find a personal trainer if necessary.
- Take up running.
- Walk with a friend.
- Find a support group to help you break a bad habit.
- Get regular checkups.
- Avoid unhealthy foods. See a nutritionist or take a nutrition class.
- Take a mental break. Meditate. Practice stress management.
- Avoid excessive alcohol and drug abuse.
- Take a vacation. Relax.
- Stop smoking or using tobacco products.
- Practice conflict resolution.
- Forgive.

Be sure to check with a medical professional before making any changes to your health plan, such as beginning an exercise program or changing your diet.

Take care of yourself. Make a healthy lifestyle a priority.

28.

Be Analytical

Problem-solving skills, a product of an analytical mind, are essential in the workplace to keep things moving smoothly. Critical thinking—the ability to analyze a situation or problem and think it through to a logical conclusion—is a key asset every employee should cultivate. Analytical thinking can aid in solving problems dealing with tasks, projects, and people. It can sort through information to find ways to increase productivity; improve products, services, and relationships; and add to personal effectiveness.

Effective critical thinking involves a passion for the topic in question. When you are passionate, your interest in learning more about the subject contributes to analyzing, drawing conclusions, and arriving at solutions.

You might be called on to use analytical skills in a variety of workplace situations. For instance, you might be given a large volume of data and be asked to analyze it, looking for specific trends to help your company remain profitable or to find new streams of income. You may be called upon to discover more efficient ways to complete a project. You may be asked to study a product to determine if it can be produced less expensively or be made to operate more efficiently. You may even be asked to resolve workplace conflicts. Any number of situations, tasks, or problems might be given to you to correct or improve.

How can you hone analytical skills? Practice. One way to use analytical skills for personal gain is to review your past performance. Analyze what is adding to your career success and what is not working. Decide what you should continue doing or what you should change. Seek ways to improve weak areas.

How can you use analytical skills to solve problems? You will need to gather information. Ask the following:

- What type of problem are you facing?
- How can you discover all the facts necessary to make a viable analysis?
- Are there any underlying issues with the problem? If so, what are they?
- How much time is allotted to you to solve the problem?
- Do you need to draw a timeline?
- What do you need to know? (This will depend on the results you expect.)
- Do you already have any of the information you need?
- Can information be easily gathered?
- Do you have the authority and the ability to collect every piece of information you need? If not, who does?
- Are you aware of any missing facts? If so, will you be able to find them or can someone give them to you?
- Are you gathering information from reliable sources?

Find the necessary sources to research your dilemma. Have you checked for hidden agendas and biases? Eliminate unreliable and skewed sources. Have you asked the right questions or do you have to backtrack to ask different questions? Do you have to dig deeper? Have you found evidence to support the information you have acquired?

Will you use individuals as your sources? You may want to gather alternative views and examine viewpoints from another's perspective. Ask appropriate questions of the right people to obtain as complete and accurate information as possible. Have you arrived at insights that will help you with your decision?

Do not assume your information is correct. Double-check facts. Validate sources to ensure accuracy, especially online sources. An error could be made in research studies, articles, interviews, and by the individuals writing the articles you cite. If you still do not have enough information to analyze the problem, where can you find additional data?

After you have gathered all information, assemble it in an organized, logical manner. Sift through the facts and identify issues related to the problem you wish to solve. You might find glaring issues or discover hidden ones. Analyze the information from all angles and break it down into manageable details. Compare, contrast, and organize the information. Evaluate differing points of view and combine perspectives to lay out a complete picture.

Take a problem apart to examine every facet. Write down pertinent points so you get a clear picture of the facts. Consider these questions:

- Have you researched the problem or similar ones?
- Do you have personal biases? (You will want to set them aside.)
- Have you looked at criteria affecting the problem and its outcome?
- What are the key issues?
- Have you compared all the information you have gathered to similar problems you have solved in the past?
- What are the reasons behind your conclusions?
- Is there evidence to support your conclusions?

Summarize what you have learned. How much are you willing to risk on your decision? Eliminate options that are riskier than you would like. Which option has the best odds of succeeding? Take the time to understand the complete picture. Have you included viewpoints other than yours? Narrow the possibilities, aiming for the most logical answer. Make an applicable decision based on the facts and your judgment and analysis. After reaching your decision, evaluate it, and then apply it.

What are the consequences of your proposed solution as you see them? What are the advantages and disadvantages? Are acceptable alternatives available? What are the alternatives? Are there key questions you still need to ask and answer? How will you deal with any negative consequences of your decision after it is implemented?

An analytical mind will help you handle complex situations through examination of acquired information and then breaking it down to identify the cause of the issue, planning corrective strategies, and taking appropriate action as you see it based on a logical conclusion. However, be aware that although you can control what you put into the decision-making process, you cannot control the outcome of your decision because there are too many unmanageable variables.

Develop critical-thinking skills by analyzing and solving problems.

29.

Be Versatile

Do your job well and take pride in your work, but be willing to adjust when necessary. Often, we get in the mindset that what we have been doing all along is the only way to accomplish the task. Maybe it is, but if a suggestion is made to change course from the usual way things have been done, do not close your mind to that possibility. There is the chance a different approach may indeed be a better one.

If you have a strong opinion about a decision that must be made and your opinion is overridden, do not take offense and close yourself off to the proposed solution. Look at the solution from all angles and consider the most beneficial elements.

If you still are in disagreement but the decision has been made by the supervisor or the team to go ahead anyway, you need to get behind the decision and put your personal opinions aside for the good of the company.

Versatile people make constant adjustments to their work, their schedules, and their interaction with others, as well as to any number of other aspects of their lives. Having the versatility to adapt quickly to these circumstances allows them to perform at top efficiency.

People who are versatile do not become discouraged when faced with adversity. They realize setbacks are part of everyone's life, and they find ways around negative situations.

Make whatever adjustments are necessary to overcome obstacles that keep you from performing at top efficiency.

30.
Take Risks

Taking risks is inevitable if you want to succeed, but you can minimize risks by looking at the big picture, emulating others who have handled similar situations, weighing possible outcomes, researching, seeking help, and using good judgment. Focus on the rewards of a positive outcome and go for it.

It may be a safe bet to do your job and not make waves, but being overly cautious will not help your career in the long run. Successful people display leadership qualities, and leaders are risk takers. Sometimes you have to put yourself or your job on the line and take a chance even when you are hesitant to do so. Without risk there are few rewards. Regardless of your position, sharpen your leadership skills by solving problems, coping positively with change, and thinking ahead. Risk takers are always looking to the future and constantly working toward meeting the changes they see coming.

Some people are afraid to move out of their comfort zones at work for fear of making mistakes, getting in over their heads, bringing notice to themselves, getting fired, or feeling discomfort. These fears can be paralyzing and hold employees back from doing their best. If fear is holding you back, ask yourself if these qualms are rational or if your negative thoughts are causing irrational doubts and resistance. Would it be worth it to challenge your fears? Even if you are not in a supervisory role, fear of failure and risk-taking could keep you from doing any job to the best of your ability. What would be the benefits of combating your fears? What would you and your company gain?

Risk takers move past their fears to take action. What is holding you back? Write down your reservations and address each one. As you realize the inconsequence of each, let it go. If the fear is valid, how can you address and overcome it? Use creative strategies that minimize the risk but provide for a new, unorthodox way of thinking. Do not become so attached to your opinions and methods that you are closed to options. Otherwise, you will stagnate and be worthless to your company.

If you worry about taking risks, ask yourself why. Is it because of a lack of skills? Take a course or otherwise hone your skills. Are you afraid you will get in over your head? Weigh the pros and cons of taking on more responsibilities. Can you reasonably handle more responsibility? If you become overwhelmed, is there someone who can help you? Engage others in your problem solving and decisions if possible. Empower others to contribute equally.

Are you afraid you will make the wrong decision? Sharpen your decision-making skills. By learning how to make good decisions, you will minimize risky outcomes. Learn how to measure uncertainty against the outcome by studying those who are successful, staying informed, and developing good judgment.

Are you afraid of change? Change is a constant in everyone's life. If you make a change in how you perform your duties, will your work life improve? What about changes in other areas of your life? Is there room for improvement? Challenge yourself to do something uncomfortable that will make your life better.

If a risk you take does not have the results you intended, learn from the experience and move on. Have an alternative plan in case the risk you take goes wrong.

One thing to keep in mind is what a company will tolerate in terms of risk—that is, what it believes is a risk worth taking with sufficient rewards versus one that is reckless.

Little is gained without risk. Weigh the possibilities and options and take a calculated risk.

31.
Be Charismatic

Charismatic people are gifted with qualities that draw others to them. They are sensitive to other people's feelings and circumstances. They are good listeners and practice empathy. Many of our great leaders have or have had charismatic personalities, which drew people to them and also influenced their thinking. These special people lead others to buy into their visions.

People want to follow charismatic people and are highly influenced by them because of their genuine interest and concern. They draw people to them with their pleasant personalities and upstanding character.

To appeal to others, treat everyone as the most important person you know. If you continue to show each individual the same consideration, you may find yourself truly caring about everyone you encounter, thereby creating a charismatic personal trait.

Charismatic people can influence others through their positive personality traits. To inspire and influence others, display behaviors that encourage people to follow you. Smile and make eye contact. Have a kind word for everyone. Compliment people when deserved. Acknowledge them each and every time you see them. Be attentive. Consistently prove you are interested in what they have to say, what they do, and how they feel.

Display sincerity at all times. People will catch on if you are faking and will avoid you rather than be pulled to you. Act professionally, maintain integrity, and be friendly and open.

Show a genuine interest in and encourage others.

PART II

INTERACTING WITH CHIEFS AND CO-WORKERS

4

PLAY NICE

I t is imperative to connect in a positive way with everyone in the workplace, from co-workers to supervisors to subordinates. Pleasant workplace relationships contribute to the type of environment where people can do their jobs in the most efficient, productive way and enjoy what they are doing.

Although you may not take a personal liking to everyone with whom you work, you must connect in a way that allows you to work alongside each other in harmony. By taking an interest in and cooperating with others, you foster constructive communication.

32.

Find Common Interests

Most people who work together are more alike than different in that they share similar feelings, interests, and desires. Basically, these people want to have a happy life, enjoy their work, and have their needs met.

One of the primary things you can do to build valued work relationships is take the time to get to know your co-workers. Discovering the personal side of co-workers will humanize them for you and humanize you for them. Find something you have in common with each person with whom you work. By befriending your co-workers, you come to know the idiosyncrasies that make them unique individuals. When you discover commonalities, you may have a tendency toward tolerance and overlooking some of the little things that might drive you crazy about them.

If you are shy, force yourself to smile and make eye contact. Your actions will encourage others to open up to you, allowing you to relate to them. Pay attention to what people talk about during lunch and breaks to find someone with interests similar to yours. This will give you an opening for a future conversation.

Sharing interests can also provide an effective escape from routine tasks. You may find your days at work to be more pleasant because of things you have in common with those around you, adding balance to what would otherwise be a one-sided work life. Having a friend to talk to at lunch not only provides a release from stress but also is enjoyable and even entertaining. Hobbies, personal interests, classes you are taking, family members, and vacations may be things you will want to share as you become friendly with co-workers. In addition to the social aspect, sharing ideas and common problems may give you a new perspective and help you through your own challenges.

Mutual interests with co-workers bind us together and put us on friendlier terms. You have to acquaint yourself with someone to bond over interests. After you connect, you may feel more kindly toward her. You may be forgiving of little irritations and inclined to show courtesy and cooperation. We are usually more tolerant of friends than strangers.

Consider this scenario: You are sitting in a long line of traffic. A car comes up alongside you with a turn signal indicating the driver would like to cut in the line in front of you. Let's say you have had a really bad day. It's hot out, your air-conditioner is broken, and you have been waiting your turn for several minutes. Under the circumstances, you are not motivated to let another driver cut in front of you. Would it make a difference to you if the other driver were a friend instead of a stranger? It probably would to most of us, and we would gesture the friend through.

Spend a little time getting to know each co-worker. You may want to learn the answers to these questions:

- Does she have a family?
- Does she have pets?
- What matters most to her?
- Does she share similar hobbies to yours—perhaps reading, scrapbooking, or gardening?
- Is she a sports enthusiast? (Of course you do not want to make the mistake of picking on her favorite team.)
- Does she participate in sports? (Maybe you have golf or bicycling in common.)
- Does she like to cook, play an instrument, or listen to music?
- Does she enjoy the same television programs or movies as you do?

Learn enough about your co-worker to know her moods and be able to read her emotions to minimize misunderstandings and problems. Try to predict the meaning she will attach to your messages before you deliver them.

All that being said, you will want to use discretion when sharing personal information. Circumstances that are too personal in nature should not be shared in the workplace, including money arguments, spousal or dating problems, personal crimes and court hearings, and the like. Avoid snooping into areas of your co-worker's personal business that you have no reason to question. Evade controversial and embarrassing subjects and situations. Such discussions can become frustrating.

If your co-worker needs someone to listen when she has a bad day, lend an ear and be sensitive to her needs. You do not have to solve her problems or give advice; just listen. If you give the impression you are sincerely interested, your co-worker may be comforted or cheered. Sometimes people just need to know someone cares about how they feel. Take care not to recite a list of your own problems or similar situations or to dominate the conversation in any way.

Express an interest in what your co-worker does at work. You do not need a detailed job description, but being interested in a co-worker's job conveys you care. A worker's self-esteem is often tied to her job. Ask thoughtful questions to engage the co-worker.

Show an interest in others and look for commonalities.

33.

Look for Co-Workers' Strengths, not Shortcomings

No one likes to be criticized, but it is easy to criticize and point out the faults of another. Sometimes we do not even have to look too hard to find these faults. Reverse the situation and reflect on a time when someone else pointed out your faults and then consider that your co-workers feel similarly when you pass judgment on them.

We fail to recognize our co-worker's feelings in our haste to point out their faults. Instead of dwelling on co-workers' weaknesses, focus on their strengths. We all have those, too. Is your co-worker a math genius? Does he have a propensity toward science? Is she awesome at resolving customer complaints? Is he dependable? Will she pitch in when the going gets tough? Is he a good listener? Does she back you on important decisions? Does she bring donuts on Fridays? The trait you focus on does not have to be outstanding or remarkable in any way. It could be as simple as someone telling you good morning in a cheerful voice every day.

Show your support for your co-worker. What are his strengths? Point those out instead of his shortcomings. Congratulate him for his achievements and praise his efforts whenever he has done something well. Peer praise makes a positive impact and encourages a team-player attitude. Promote your co-worker's agenda and help her achieve her goals. This will indicate that you feel she and her job are important.

Contribute to positive office morale through an enthusiastic attitude and a desire to complete your share of tasks and company projects as well as put forth a team effort. You do not have to like everyone you work with, but you must be able to get along well enough to complete the job.

Look for the good in people. Catch your co-worker doing something positive and commend him.

34.

Show Appreciation for What Co-Workers Do for You

How many times have you performed a favor for a co-worker and not been thanked? Have you ever helped someone out and been ignored afterward? If either happened to you, it probably did not leave you with a warm, fuzzy feeling. You may have felt taken advantage of. In fact, you may even have decided not to support that person in the future. Now, reverse the situation and think of the times your co-workers did something for you. Did you remember to thank them properly? If not, is it too late to give them a general thank-you for all their past assistance?

It is important to let co-workers know you appreciate the favors they do for you, whether personal or in a work capacity. You do not have to provide a gift or go overboard with your appreciation. Even a simple word of thanks goes a long way when responding to a favor or kindness. Say thank you with a genuine smile. Another way to show gratitude to co-workers is to offer to assist them in the future when they need it. Again, do it with a smile and sincere willingness.

Acknowledging a co-worker's thoughtfulness is a common courtesy often over-looked because we have come to rely on people helping us on the job. We can become complacent in showing our appreciation, especially when we feel we are entitled to a co-worker's help. We often forget he is not *required* to help us do our job. A verbal or written thank-you, depending on the situation, should always be at the ready.

It does not take a parade in our honor to make us feel valued. A pat on the back can often have the same effect. Small gestures of appreciation can have a big impact and leave lasting impressions—for example, bringing donuts or other goodies to work, buying your co-worker an espresso, giving her a card, or buying her lunch.

Other ways to appreciate co-workers are by recognizing birthdays and other special occasions, the completion of a special project, life-changing events, and achievements in their lives. These can be business or personal situations. Such recognition solidifies bonds and creates satisfying work relationships.

When the situation is reversed and you have supported a co-worker in some way, do not automatically expect him to thank you, even though thanks would be the proper action. You may come to resent him if your expected thank-you is not forth-coming. It is better not have expectations when you offer to help co-workers.

Tell co-workers you appreciate them.

35.
Work with, Not Against, Co-Workers

How do you feel when you have to deal with someone who is argumentative, whiny, inefficient, and generally miserable? You probably feel the same way anyone would when confronted with such a personality: You want to avoid the person. Do your part to establish the type of personality that does not repel co-workers or anyone else.

Getting along with co-workers is not merely an option; it is a *requirement* if you want to have a rewarding career. All employees must work together to be successful and to bring success to their companies. Someone may have an attitude, character traits, and a working style different from yours, but that does not mean you cannot get along.

One way to be cooperative and to get co-workers to cooperate with you in return is to treat them with courtesy and respect at all times. Do what you can to make people feel comfortable in your presence. Watch what you say and do, remaining professional at all times. Listen to their comments and questions.

Accept people as they are, not as you want them to be. Respect their rights. Give and take is a part of every relationship, and office associations are no different. Cooperative effort allows people to get the job done more efficiently.

Cooperate fully with co-workers, training yourself to be someone with whom people want to associate. Be polite and work hard not to cause problems with co-workers. Never lie or gossip to get ahead. Do not show off or tease and play jokes on another co-worker, especially to make an impression on the boss or other co-workers.

Trust co-workers enough to do their jobs so you are free to do yours even better. Trust motivates people and creates benefits for the entire workplace. Do your part to establish an environment where co-workers are encouraged and empowered. Morale is higher when people perform in a satisfying environment.

Unless it is your responsibility, withhold negative criticism, especially if it is about something that has no bearing on work. Criticism regarding how co-workers do their jobs or interact with others should include positive suggestions for improvement. The same is true for criticism of work habits.

When you work on team projects, follow these suggestions:

- Take the initiative.
- Volunteer for tasks.
- Do your share of the work.
- Take pride in your work.
- Help co-workers complete their tasks.
- Be cooperative and professional, particularly if you expect others to act that way.
- Inspire co-workers to do their best work by setting a good example.
- Encourage creativity. Everyone should be given the opportunity to contribute ideas in an inviting environment.
- Acknowledge and respect co-workers for their individual uniqueness and contributions.
- Learn from everyone involved.

If you are in a position to lead co-workers, challenge them to be creative and hard working. Be a mentor; help those just starting out. Keep the lines of communication open and encourage questions. Pass on your expertise and delegate responsibilities to others who are qualified. Initiate an open-door policy where people will not be afraid to approach you. Express your appreciation for the work they do.

People who are cooperative share these traits:

- They do their job well.
- They are loyal to those around them.
- They do not let co-workers down.
- They always keep their word.
- They hold up their end of the work.

Resolve office conflicts quickly to prevent negative attitudes, hard feelings, and problems from escalating. Listen to your co-workers' opinions and thoughts on the conflict. Remain calm and reasonable. Be sensitive to your co-workers' feelings, needs, and situations. Make a list of positive and negative input and look for a solution that would be fair to all parties. If you cannot resolve the issues among yourselves, consider asking a third party to mediate. Try to resolve problems before going to the supervisor. Running to a supervisor could be construed as immature and a waste of valuable work time.

Maintain objectivity when dealing with co-workers and treat everyone with fairness. Avoid favoritism. Showing favoritism toward certain co-workers can create an uncomfortable, adverse environment where people feel offended, let down, and discriminated against. This is particularly true for those in supervisory positions who show favoritism.

If you are in a supervisory position, take care to be above reproach when it comes to hiring. Always hire and promote the most qualified candidate based on objectivity. Differences in status create barriers that influence how well individuals communicate. A subordinate may not be inclined to be upfront with a superior because of fear of retaliation, job loss, or even wariness. Supervisors often manipulate subordinates consciously or subconsciously when they should be empowering subordinates and equipping them with the information and tools they need to do their jobs.

Opposites have always had to work together. Some people have messy desks, while others are organized. Some are outgoing and strong-willed, while others are quiet and introverted. One co-worker might be a go-getter who completes tasks quickly and efficiently, while another may plod along barely getting by. Age plays a part with young and old working together, and those from different cultures bring their own customs and values. Ethics, character traits, learning styles, habits, and the like create diversity in the workplace.

This diversity should be addressed in a positive way to encourage cooperation and sharing of individual talents and ideas. All employees must be motivated to work together in harmony to meet company goals. Recognize that differences are just that and should not be a factor that sets one employee against another.

Be sensitive to co-workers' moods. Everyone has a bad day occasionally. Show that you care about their feelings. Do not take things the wrong way, which results in hurt feelings and misconceptions that ruin relationships.

Do your part to get along with everyone in the workplace.

36.

Avoid Listening to Gossip and Spreading Rumors

The informal gossip chain in a company, also known as the office grapevine, transmits messages rapidly from person to person. However, the messages are often false and unfounded. Add to that the fact some people will embellish the gossip or even twist the facts to meet their own purpose before passing the rumor along to others. Before you know it, false statements and incorrect information are disseminated among workers with alarming speed.

If gossip negatively affects them, workers suffer from the toll it takes on their emotions in a number of ways including anger, frustration, confusion, shock, stress, and hurt feelings. When rumors about layoffs, changes in policy, transfers, personal problems, and the like spread through the grapevine, they are difficult to stop.

Do not originate, contribute to, or circulate gossip and rumors you hear. In addition to causing grief among co-workers, sharing unfounded hearsay could land you in a lot of trouble with the boss. Your participation in spreading rumors could create a hostile work environment, cause morale to plummet, reduce productivity, or divulge confidential information—all causes for reprimand or dismissal.

Gossipers are looked upon as troublemakers and are considered untrustworthy. Disengage from conversations with these individuals. People who spread gossip attach themselves to anyone who will listen. They often distort their tales. Why listen to information that may be false or rumors of things that might never come to pass? Be wise and ignore rumormongers.

Do your part to squelch unfounded rumors about the company, your supervisor, and your co-workers. Negative tales about company policies could lower or hinder productivity if employees become stressed, angry, or apathetic because of what they have heard. Although you will not shut down the rumor mill simply by not participating, you will have done your duty by keeping the environment positive.

On an encouraging note, office gossip can be enlightening when it is conveyed in a constructive manner, as in when co-workers informally share the latest news, provide solutions to problems, and share what they like about the company without any malicious comments.

Gossip causes ill feelings, misunderstandings, and a number of other problems. Avoid gossiping and those who spread gossip.

37.

Set Boundaries

Do co-workers often interrupt you? Do they overstay their welcome? Does your supervisor rant? If so, you may need to set boundaries. Some people do not realize they are being disrespectful of your time; others do not care that they are disruptive and taking liberties.

When your thoughts are constantly interrupted by a bothersome co-worker, you must establish clear guidelines to protect your time. Work should be a priority, so it is appropriate to tell a co-worker you need quiet to focus on a task and finish it.

As you see an annoying co-worker approach, find a way to make yourself look busy. You can keep your eyes on your work and refuse to look at the interrupter, but if the person does not take the hint, you will have to speak up. Let the person know you are too busy to stop and talk right now. Say, "I'm sorry, but I have an important project due," or "That sound interesting. Could we discuss it at lunch when I will have more time?"

Occasionally a co-worker or supervisor will attempt to take advantage of you, especially if you are shy or non-confrontational. Be a team player, but decide now that you will not allow anyone to take advantage of you.

Set boundaries for negative behaviors you encounter in the workplace. Again, your co-worker or supervisor may be unaware he is being obnoxious, or he may not care that he is. Make him aware of the problem in a peaceable manner. If that fails to correct the problem, you may have to voice your concerns using firm statements. Say, "I find that behavior unacceptable," or "That language is inappropriate in the workplace," or "I would appreciate your asking before borrowing my supplies." Certain situations demand that you tell an offensive person in no uncertain terms you will not accept this behavior.

You will develop personal relationships in the workplace and must decide what type of boundaries you want to set in that area. For instance, will you share personal details of your life? Will you tell co-workers about your family, relationships, home life, education, and finances? How much will you share? What areas will be off limits? How will you maintain these boundaries when co-workers who are now your friends cross the line? How will you define the work relationship with your supervisor?

How will you enforce workforce boundaries? How do you keep co-workers from invading your space? How will you avoid being drawn into office dramas? You may have to walk away from unprofessional conversations. If co-workers continue to cross the boundaries after you have set them, you may need to keep supplies and personal belongings in locked drawers and cabinets, close your office door, or hang a sign on your doorknob asking not to be disturbed.

What workplace boundaries will you set? Following are some common problems where co-workers and others have overstepped the boundaries of common courtesy.

Set boundaries for people who:

- Walk into your office unannounced and interrupt your work
- Go into your desk drawers or rummage on the top of your desk without your permission
- Take your supplies without asking
- Stand at your desk and chatter while you are trying to work
- Steal lunches
- Steal your ideas
- Ask extremely personal questions
- Share extremely personal information
- Play music at a disturbing volume
- Make noises, crack gum, talk to themselves, etc.
- Take over your personal space
- Have loud personal phone conversations
- Finish your sentences
- Argue vehemently with you
- Shout at you

Maintaining mutual respect is important and leads to a cooperative environment. Respect the boundaries co-workers set.

Set personal and professional boundaries in the workplace. Respect other people's boundaries.

38.
Be Prepared for Meetings

Efficient meetings do not just happen. Rather, they take time and planning. Whether you are attending a meeting or planning it, you have certain responsibilities.

Attending Meetings

If you are called to attend a meeting, have the materials you will need. Anticipate your role at the meeting. Add to the discussion, but do not monopolize it or ramble on and waste everyone's time. Listen to others with an open mind.

Coordinating Meetings

If you are coordinating the meeting, be clear on the specifics: Who? What? When? Where? Why? Know the meeting topic and how the meeting involves you and the other attendees. You may have to accommodate the schedules of other people, but do not leave the meeting up to chance. Create a plan and break the planning steps down according to a timeline. Be sure to have all the details so you can develop an appropriate strategy.

If you are running the meeting, you are in a position to choose the most convenient time and the place where you are most comfortable and less likely to be distracted. Create an agenda and distribute it ahead of time so participants can be prepared. Stick to the agenda during the meeting to stay on task.

- Start on time.
- Encourage open communication and listen.
- Keep attendees on track.
- Prevent any one individual from monopolizing the discussion.
- Brush up on the subject of the meeting and anticipate questions.
- Have appropriate materials available.

Giving Presentations

If you are giving a presentation, be thoroughly prepared with the material and learn something about your audience members so you can relate to them. Check equipment ahead of time and be familiar with the technology you plan to use.

Write down the main points you want people to remember from your presentation. Keep them in front of you throughout your talk. Make your point first and then offer a comment or explanation. Stress important points and underscore their importance through emphasis. Do not rush through information; think about what you want to say and consider your words carefully.

Give attendees time to absorb information by pausing a few seconds between key points. Communicate at a level appropriate for attendees and use jargon judiciously. Make your presentation interesting and entertaining. Be accessible to your audience by moving around the room and making eye contact instead of standing at a podium or reading from your notes. Use gestures to reinforce your message, but avoid nervous movements.

Allow time for questions and encourage participation if suitable. When answering questions, it is fine to say you need a moment to think about the answer rather than give an incorrect or incomplete answer. If you do not have time to answer questions during the presentation, make yourself available afterward.

Use visuals properly. If you have PowerPoint slides and/or hard-copy handouts, be prepared to distribute them digitally to attendees. Give the audience more information than what is on the slide rather than reading directly from it.

Here are some tips:

- Decide what to say ahead of time. Speaking without advanced preparation weakens a presentation.
- Practice beforehand.
- Start on time.
- Have an outline or notecards with important points. Stay focused.
- Use clear, easy-to-understand language. Be specific.
- Use proper grammar and pronunciation.
- Look at your audience.
- Watch nonverbal appearance and mannerisms.
- Be sincere.
- Prepare visuals—PowerPoint presentations, handouts, demonstrations, etc.
- Allow time for questions.

Be prepared whether you are coordinating a meeting or merely attending one.

39.
Don't Give Unsolicited Advice

When you feel you know a better way of handling things, it is tempting to tell your co-worker how he should manage a certain situation or deal with a problem. However, it is best not to give unsolicited advice, which is often unwanted, unless you are the boss.

Assuming you are not their supervisor, do not attempt to advise co-workers, especially those on the same level as you. If you feel an urge to manage someone or the situation in which they are involved, remind yourself that adults do not want to be controlled. They will especially take offense when the person attempting to manage them is not in charge. When supervising others, do so in a way that leads or directs them rather than one that micromanages or commands them.

Unless it is your job to do so or a co-worker specifically asks for your help, refrain from telling co-workers what to do or how to do a task. You may think you are doing the co-worker a favor by advising him, but that way of thinking may backfire if he sees it as interference or an invasion of his domain. If your co-worker feels he is doing a proper job and you are not in charge of him or what he is doing, he may see your comments as negative criticism or a know-it-all attitude. Telling someone else how to do his job could be construed as overstepping boundaries.

In addition to resenting uninvited advice, many people are on information overload these days and do not want to be saddled with opinions they feel will not contribute to making their job easier or improving their situation.

Sometimes, however, you must give advice. For instance, you may have knowledge of how to handle a repeat customer that would benefit a co-worker who must deal with him. Or maybe you know the boss likes the sales figures compiled a certain way and your co-worker has unknowingly compiled them in a different format.

In such cases, be careful about the way you impart the information to co-workers even if it is your responsibility to do so. Be helpful but do not act like you know everything, even if you feel you do. Know-it-alls are not regarded positively, especially when they try to force their knowledge on others. Consider your co-worker's mood. If he does not seem receptive, he probably will not accept your advice and may even resent it. Be aware of his nonverbal cues. Does he seem open to your suggestions or does he seem to take offense? Wait until he is in an open-minded mood if possible.

Limit your comments to work-related items. Not everyone wants to know how you feel about all subjects or situations, especially when they do not concern them or their jobs. It is best to steer clear of personal conversations altogether unless your opinion is expressly solicited, and then you would be wise to speak carefully.

If you are in a supervisory position, lead your employees rather than bossing or pushing them to complete their work. It is easier for people to accept information if it does not seem like an order. Without being condescending, stress the benefit to the subordinate of following your advice or directive. Sometimes you can word information so the co-worker thinks the advice or suggestion you are giving is her idea.

Hold participative meetings where everyone can freely contribute information and opinions and ask questions. Criticize or reprimand in private. If you must give unsolicited advice to resolve a behavior or other problem, be sensitive to the person's feelings. Take her aside to a private place and choose words carefully. Using "I" statements and offering examples of your own past errors will show her that everyone makes mistakes now and then. Point out that you are trying to help the person become a better worker or form rewarding work relationships.

One type of advice most people appreciate is positive feedback. People want meaningful feedback that reinforces the job they are doing. As a supervisor, let them know they are performing up to standards or are going above and beyond. You may want to relay comments you feel would be helpful. If employees are not doing satisfactory work, let them know how they can improve themselves and their work.

Think carefully before giving unsolicited advice. Be helpful but not presumptuous.

40.

Be Approachable

Have you ever worked with someone who is rude, obnoxious, or just plain mean? How did you feel whenever you had to approach this person to get information to complete your job or work on the same team or share an office or lunchroom? Most people would cringe at the thought. These openly aggressive co-workers make life difficult for everyone else. The work must be done in spite of the bad behavior, which forces co-workers to put up with the conduct. These troublemakers demoralize their co-workers, who then wonder why they must be subjected to undesirables in shared office spaces. Stress and hard feelings ensue.

People who are not outright hostile but are uninviting contribute to an unwelcoming atmosphere. A dour, unfriendly expression will be standoffish to co-workers. No one wants to deal with uncooperative, short-tempered, and unpleasant co-workers. To maintain a hospitable work environment, you must be pleasant and approachable all the time. Have an open, sincere manner.

A daily dose of ill behavior will give you a reputation as someone others will want to avoid at all costs. Constant bad behavior and a poor attitude will probably get you fired. Employers strive to find employees who will work well together.

One instance of grumpy, rude, or offensive behavior may also have a negative impact on your reputation. However, people will be more forgiving of an isolated instance, especially if you apologize. People understand that everyone has an occasional bad day.

It is every employee's responsibility to build harmony in the workplace. Something simple anyone can do to be approachable is to have a genuine smile for everyone. Even if you are shy, you can offer a smile.

Set a good example for others. Cooperation, courtesy, and tact in dealing with people are essential. Engage co-workers in pleasant conversations and try to include everyone. Be friendly, but not too social.

Loyalty and keeping confidences in the workplace are two hugely important traits. When people know they can trust you to keep their secrets and to stand by them in all situations, they are more likely to approach you with their concerns and open up to you. Never undermine their trust and confidence in you.

Let others know they can come to you with questions and when they need help with a project or other task. Never imply they are stupid or embarrass them. Also, be open to their opinions.

Pay attention to your body language, which speaks volumes. Crossed arms and avoiding eye contact when speaking to someone will give the sense you are closed off. Be inviting by smiling, making eye contact (but not staring), and having a relaxed demeanor. Compliment people to boost their self-confidence, but do not overdo it as that may be seen as insincere.

Some additional ways to be more approachable include the following:

- Be pleasant and friendly.
- Extend common courtesies.
- Be respectful.
- Acknowledge your co-workers in a positive way.
- Show a genuine interest in others.
- Do not exclude anyone.
- Be willing to listen more than you speak.
- Have a positive attitude. Avoid moodiness.

If you become emotional, strive to remain calm and in control. Expressing frustration and anger through crying, shouting, or stomping away will repel co-workers.

When you must deal with negative behavior in the workplace, find a way to adjust to the behavior or ignore it. Can you avoid the person in question? Can you do your job without the person's help? If so, concentrate on doing your job. If you need to work with the negative person, can you sit down and discuss the behavior in a non-threatening way? If you cannot resolve the situation, you may have to bring the behavior to the attention of your supervisor.

Make sure your behavior is sending the right message: I am approachable and will treat you with respect.

41.

Be Tolerant of Co-Workers' Work Habits

Not everyone will have the same work style as you do. Personalities, habits, learning styles, training, and background are some of the things that affect work style. Even the setup of a workspace contributes to how a person does her work.

We may question why our co-worker does what she does and says what she says. We ask questions like these:

- Why does she act the way she does?
- Why is she not more like me?
- Why is her desk always a mess?
- Why is she late for meetings?
- Why does she not start projects as soon as they are assigned?
- Why can't she see she is doing things all wrong?
- What makes her think that could possibly work?
- When is she going to do things the right way?
- Where does she come up with her crazy ideas?

The first thing to realize is not everyone thinks and acts the same way. Your co-worker's messy desk is not an automatic indication she is inefficient. She may be of a different personality type than you are, and that personality type could be efficient amid all the chaos.

Rather than judge another person's method of operation, accept and adjust to it. You do not have to change your own work habits and should not expect other people to change theirs. Be understanding, supportive, and tolerant of others' habits.

If a co-worker's work habits are intolerable, you may want to discuss the situation with him. Be aware, though, of his right to work as he wants—as long as he is performing his duties satisfactorily and is not interfering with your work. Maybe he works well in his messy area. Preaching to someone about how he should clean up his work area usually does not remedy the situation. Of course, you can offer suggestions and helpful tips, but do not expect the person to do as you say.

Organize your work habits around the talents and personality traits of your co-workers. Complete your part of the project in your own office. If you share an office, turn your desk around so you do not have to look as his messy one. If you can put a divider between your desks, that is even better.

If a co-worker's actual performance is up to par, perhaps his work habits are irrelevant in the big picture. Try to understand why your co-worker does what he does. Create an environment where he can work according to his habits and preferences.

Remember that people are unique and as such may behave and think differently than you do. Find a way to work together.

42.

Look at the Situation from the Co-Worker's Viewpoint

We all have a tendency to believe we are right in what we do, say, and think. When we have this belief, we tend to think others, such as co-workers, are in the wrong. We may question a co-worker's words and actions, but sometimes we need to step back and look at things the way he sees them. After all, he believes he is right, too.

Your co-worker may be operating from a vantage point you know nothing about but that changes his perception of the situation in a way that affects his thoughts and behavior. If you take the time to listen to him or to look at things the way he does, you may change your opinion or at the very least understand where he is coming from. This simple understanding may lead to tolerance or acceptance.

It is all right if you do not accept your co-worker's point of view, but be considerate of his right to that view.

Everything is not always as it looks from your perspective. Consider the other person's viewpoint.

43.

Focus on Your Own Work

Too many people are worried about what the person next to them is doing, what he might be getting away with, or what extra privileges he is receiving. Placing your attention on your co-worker's business takes the focus from your own work. Focusing too much on a co-worker's actions and behavior could also lead to mistaken beliefs that escalate and damage work relationships and hinder productivity. If you have enough time to worry about what your co-worker is doing, consider asking for additional responsibilities so your time is better spent.

If you feel your co-worker is not pulling his weight, you might try asking him to help you with your duties. If he is unwilling to help or hints that he is too busy, you may have to resign yourself to that fact and concentrate on your job so you do not become jaded. If a serious problem arises with a co-worker (for example, something illegal), you should take your concerns to your supervisor if you feel it is a danger to yourself, your co-workers, or your company.

Place your attention on your work and your skills. By concentrating on yourself, you can do what is necessary to further your career. Keep a record of everything you do at work. The record will reinforce your belief that you are doing your part to attain professional success and the success of your company. In addition, you will have a written record of your accomplishments to show your supervisor during evaluations of your job performance. This will show you are making the most of your time.

Concentrate on improving yourself rather than worrying about your co-worker's business.

44.

Stay on Task

Self-sabotaging behavior like procrastination will rob you of time and a sense of accomplishment and is detrimental to career success. Unfortunately, it is easy to procrastinate because putting things off until later or not doing them at all can feel rewarding in itself.

Companies count on productive employees to keep the business operating. Your unproductive days affect the entire company.

If you have trouble staying on task, recognize you have a problem and find ways to overcome it. At the very least, commit to starting the task at hand. Once you do that, you may find yourself so immersed in the job you end up finishing it. If you do not finish the project, at least you will have part of it completed. This may be the encouragement you need to continue.

Any progress you make could be an incentive to do the work and eliminate excuses. Consistent, diligent action will lead to progress, even if you are only taking small steps.

Many people try to multi-task when they should be single-minded. Divided attention is often a distraction and not the most effective way of working. Put aside all work but the task at hand. It often requires complete focus to overcome challenges or problems.

Focus your efforts on completing each task as effectively as possible.

5

CONTRIBUTE TO A
POSITIVE WORK
ENVIRONMENT

Everybody wins when the environment in which he or she works is positive and harmonious. Each employee has a responsibility to uphold this harmony. Good habits, common courtesy, and solid professional ethics lay a sound foundation for a constructive workplace. Do your part to minimize discord. Exhibit personal characteristics that are conducive to a productive environment. Your success and that of your company depend on cooperative, professional behavior.

45.

Mind Your Own Business

Just as you would not want someone snooping in your business, whether work or personal, you should not pry into other people's affairs. Eavesdropping is an intrusion of privacy. Maintain the right to privacy for every individual in the workplace and for anyone else with whom you do business. Do not be the type of person who concerns himself with what other people are doing and saying.

People who strive to know every detail of their co-workers' personal business often become workplace snoops and gossips. They love to share whatever details they uncover. If a co-worker tries to draw you into gossip or a chat that involves confidential or unsubstantiated information, excuse yourself from the conversation. Having knowledge of confidential information that you have no business knowing could be detrimental to you if you accidentally let it slip. Such an indiscretion could make trouble for you and all parties involved. If the blunder is serious enough, it could even cost you your career.

Refrain from looking over an individual's shoulder while he performs tasks. Files, documents, and computer screens are off limits to everyone but those individuals who have business with them. Mail should be opened and read by the addressee only. In addition, do not listen in on conversations with the intention of learning others' business. Confidential information you inadvertently come across should never be discussed with anyone else.

Additionally, do not interrupt or enter into discussions between co-workers when you have not been invited. Give space to individuals you observe engaged in a private exchange and refrain from commenting to them or straining to hear their conversation. If their exchange becomes hostile, follow company procedures for reporting the incident.

When you do overhear a confidential conversation, disengage as soon as possible and do not repeat anything you heard. If the co-worker was speaking loudly in a non-private area, you may wish to advise him that his conversation could be overheard by others.

Your supervisor has the right to privacy, and should not be eavesdropped on by you or any other person at work. You may wish to know what your boss is talking about when he is in a private meeting or on a private call, but refrain from prying. The same goes for any of his other business.

Never go through company personnel files to learn confidential information about another employee. Avoid trying to find out the names of your co-worker's visitors, anyone with whom he speaks or the nature of his messages, or anything else about him or his work that does not concern you. Salaries should never be discussed, nor should you attempt to learn a co-worker's salary by viewing his paycheck or pay stub or by asking others in the company. It is unprofessional and unethical to put co-workers on the spot by asking them to divulge confidential information about the company, their (or your) job, or other co-workers.

Confidential files and paperwork or computer screens on which you are working should be shielded from view of unauthorized individuals. Take precautions against those who would eavesdrop on your conversations. Safeguard the information in employees' files of which you are in charge. Be especially diligent in guarding your supervisor's privacy and his confidential materials.

Respect the right to privacy in the workplace.

46.

Do Not Harass or Discriminate Against Co-Workers

Laws prohibit many types of harassment and discrimination. Individuals cannot be discriminated against because of their race, religion, gender, age, national origin, disability, and the like. Men and women must receive equal pay for equal work. Laws protect against sexual harassment, which includes unwelcome advances and requests for sexual favors.

Anything you do or say that makes another person feel uncomfortable or threatened can be considered harassment. You may feel your jokes and playful attitude are harmless, but if your co-worker or employer thinks they are distasteful or hateful and is offended by them, you are guilty of harassment. This includes general comments and references to a particular sex. Immediately cease the behavior and apologize. If you have displayed a picture of something offensive, take it down.

Most companies have no tolerance for people who harass or discriminate. If you are guilty of discrimination, you may be reprimanded or fired. You may even be held accountable in a court of law, as might the company for which you work. Even if certain types of discrimination are not illegal, they could be unethical. For instance, hiring a relative or a friend when another candidate is more qualified is unethical. Not hiring someone who is overweight or because of unflattering physical characteristics is also unethical. Hiring professionals should always hire the best qualified candidate, using objective criteria. Favoritism is another unethical form of discrimination.

Take care in your treatment of everyone. Bullying should not be tolerated in the workplace or anywhere else. Never show any type of open hostility, either verbally or written, that may be construed as harassment or bullying. The Internet has created new ways to harass and bully people through social media sites. Never post anything on these sites that may harm or insult anyone or be offensive in any way. Take care not to post anything that may damage your or someone else's reputation or in any way incriminate you.

You have rights when you are discriminated against. Follow your company's procedure in reporting the incident to the proper personnel. Keep a written record for yourself. If you do not obtain satisfaction, report the offense to the appropriate government agency. Laws protect against retaliation for reporting discrimination or harassment.

Become familiar with company policies and the laws on harassment and discrimination. Adhere to these laws and policies.

47.

Do Not Give Co-Workers a Reason to Complain About You

Awareness of things you say or do that cause others to find fault with you will present an opportunity for you to correct the behavior and improve work relationships. If you find your co-workers are avoiding you, check your behavior. Are you treating everyone fairly and professionally? Are you doing anything offensive on purpose or unintentionally? Did you contribute to a co-worker's distress, frustration, or anger? Is there a way to placate him? Monitor your behavior and act responsibly to have a positive impact in the workplace.

By treating everyone with respect, remaining professional at all times, and displaying effective personal traits, you minimize the chances that co-workers will complain about you in the first place. Avoid alienating co-workers with unprincipled, rude, or overbearing behavior. Do not create an uncomfortable situation for others with moodiness, outbursts, or displays of anger. Curtail conflicts by controlling personal anger and aggression.

Keep the lines of communication open. Clearly state your messages; sending contradictory messages could cause misunderstandings. Listen to people when they have something to contribute and respond when appropriate, preferably in a beneficial manner.

Filter your thoughts before speaking. It is never a good idea to say what you think if it is insulting, rude, or untrue. Without filtering, you may blurt out something that would be better left unsaid. Never demean, criticize, or yell at anyone else. This is doubly inexcusable when you have an audience. You will not be able to take back words spoken.

Be empathetic and sensitive to others. Recognize their needs. Show happiness for people when they are celebrating and sympathy when they are sorrowful. Try to understand things from the other person's perspective.

Do you resent your co-workers' actions? Resentment contributes to hostility, animosity, and co-workers avoiding you. Find a way to rise above this indignation. Can you discuss the offending actions with the co-worker in a nonthreatening manner? Can an impartial co-worker act as a go-between?

If you have a disagreement or personality conflict with a co-worker, maintain a professional demeanor around him. Ignore his attempts to irritate you. Do what you can to smooth any friction, realizing you must get along in the workplace. Can you avoid this person? Can you find something in common with him? What would it take for you to befriend him? In what way can you put differences aside and work together?

If you have a conflict with one co-worker, it may indicate a personal difference. If you find yourself embroiled in conflicts with several co-workers, it may signal a bigger problem and should find you checking your own behavior for negative traits. Are your co-workers' complaints valid? Could you be annoying co-workers without realizing it? Have you behaved in an unacceptable manner? Do you contribute to discord or create tension in your workplace?

It is never acceptable to shout or to have a tantrum in the office or attack another person verbally or physically. Tame your temper so as not to generate controversy and make trouble for yourself.

Always do you part when you are assigned tasks that involve others. No one wants to work with a slacker.

Form positive work relationships by doing the following:

- Be kind to others.
- Be friendly and sincere.
- Be honest.
- Respect boundaries.
- Display courtesy and professionalism.
- Don't complain.
- Keep uncomplimentary comments to yourself.
- Perform your job to the best of your ability.
- Follow all company policies.
- Do not take or borrow anything that does not belong to you.
- Accept blame when you are at fault.
- Do not dominate co-workers.

Behave in such a way that people will have nothing to complain about when it comes to you.

48.
Step Up and Volunteer

Anytime you volunteer to go above and beyond your normal duties to help co-workers, chiefs, and customers, you demonstrate team spirit. Volunteerism shows a consideration for the needs of others and an exceptional dedication to your career and your company.

If you have free time on your hands, pay it forward by helping a co-worker. Is the co-worker stressing over a project? Can you do something to minimize her stress? Are you willing to partner with her to finish the job? Are you qualified to help with the task? Can you take over routine tasks for a time so she can catch up on her work?

Often an individual will not expressly ask for help because she does not want to appear incompetent. Assure her you know she can handle the project but you have free time to spare and do not mind lending a hand. Never undermine her efforts.

When you need assistance in the future, a co-worker you helped might return the favor, but do not make that a consideration when you volunteer. Do it because it is the right thing to do and because it takes your professionalism up a notch.

When you are assigned a team project, volunteer to take on your share or more of the work. No one wants to do an unpleasant part of a project, but someone must. If you are capable and available, volunteer. You will be recognized as a leader who can be counted on to get the job done. Your take-charge attitude may bring additional career opportunities your way.

Individuals who go above and beyond their job duties stand out to management. In addition, helping a co-worker wins her gratitude.

Your volunteerism should not have any ulterior motives, like trying to overshadow a co-worker, to point out her incompetency, or to take credit for her ideas or her work.

If someone has to do the job, why not you?

49.

Clean Up after Yourself

Have you ever opened the lunchroom refrigerator to find containers with fuzzy contents? Have you opened the microwave and been disgusted by spills or baked-on food? Have you sat at a sticky lunchroom table or one cluttered with crumbs, castoff wrappers, dirty dishes, or objects that do not belong? Have you walked into a filthy, unsanitary restroom?

A major pet peeve in the workplace is working with co-workers who do not clean up after themselves. Thoughtless people annoy with a self-centered attitude that compels others to clean their messes. Wipe crumbs and spills you cause and pick up your belongings.

Company equipment, appliances, or furniture that is shared has a certain etiquette attached to it. For instance, if you share a microwave, refrigerator, coffee pot, and the like, abide by the accepted procedure for using and cleaning them. When your food spills over in the microwave, wipe it up. If you store your lunch in the refrigerator, take the remainder of your food and your containers home every day. Coffee drinkers should make a new pot when they empty it, take turns with co-workers cleaning the coffee pot, and contribute to the coffee fund.

Never place dirty dishes, silverware, and other items to soak in the lunchroom sink and forget about them. Do not leave items on counters where others have to work around them. Wash all items and put them away. Never leave half-filled coffee or tea cups or half-empty soda cans sitting around.

Neatly return all supplies to their places after using them. Close cupboard doors and drawers. If you use the last of any supplies, such as cream or sugar, paper towels, dish detergent, or hand soap, replace them from the supplies cabinet or tell the person in charge.

If you spill something on the table, counter, floor, or elsewhere, call maintenance or clean it up. A spill or mess could cause a fall or other accident. Even when you have a company cleaning crew, it is poor manners to leave the spill for an entire day. It is also unsafe.

If you share printers and fax machines, do not leave the machines with a paper jam. Fix paper jams and replace ink cartridges as needed or contact the person in charge. Refill paper when you use the last of it in the tray. Pick up all copies, extra papers, paperclips, and used staples. Throw away trash. If you use the last of the supplies in this area, replace them or alert the person in charge of ordering them. For instance, if the stapler needs to be refilled in the copier, replace the staples or let someone know. Staplers, three-hole punches, scissors, paper cutters, and the like should not be removed from the shared areas where they are kept.

Sharing office spaces requires co-workers to adapt to a variety of work habits. Your flexibility and thoughtfulness will contribute to an amicable environment. Keep your area neat and clean, and do not help yourself to another's things. Be considerate while sharing space, supplies, equipment, and information.

Treat all office spaces with respect. Keep all areas clean.

50.
Be on Time...for Everything

Be punctual for work every day. Chronic lateness contributes to lost time and productivity, costing companies a significant amount of money. Being late by even five minutes a day adds up over time. Co-workers who must constantly cover for your absences come to resent doing extra work while you ignore company policies.

Planning the night before will save time and frustration in the morning. Decide what you will wear to work (and make sure it is pressed), pack your lunch, gather everything you want to take with you, help family members get ready, and place your keys and personal belongings in a convenient place. You may want to set your alarm to get up earlier if you are still late.

When you arrive at work, begin your tasks. Do not waste time eating a breakfast that should have been consumed on your own time, checking personal email and social media sites, or chatting with co-workers. Return from lunch and breaks on time.

Manage your schedule so you are on time for meetings. Habitually late people send the message that they do not care about their responsibilities and have little regard for anyone else. They seem disorganized and unprofessional. Chronic lateness to meetings and for group assignments is disrespectful of other people's time. Lateness is an inconvenience that may extend the meeting time, which further impedes attendees' schedules.

Prepare ahead of time. Check your electronic and paper calendars every day or even the night before to be sure you will not miss something important. Set electronic calendars to send you an auto reminder. Gather files, compile figures, check equipment, etc., in advance. When a meeting ends, do not stay to socialize, but return to your duties.

Meet all deadlines. Figure out how your time is spent and how long it takes to do your tasks. Allow for interruptions, meetings, phone calls, and email. Keep a daily to-do list and consult it frequently. Break large projects into smaller tasks and set deadlines for those tasks. Eliminate excuses. Do the job and finish on time.

Positive time-management behaviors include the following:

- Using a to-do list
- Checking your electronic calendar
- Using the telephone
- Returning from lunch and breaks on time
- Planning

Negative time-management behaviors include the following:

- Chronic lateness
- Socializing with co-workers
- Avoiding work
- Missing deadlines

Be respectful of your and everyone else's time.

51.
Use Proper Phone Etiquette

Ideally, business calls should be made from office phones, not personal mobile phones. Regardless of how calls are made, consideration must be shown to those around you. A ringing phone disturbs those who may be trying to focus on tasks and interrupts people who are having meetings or conversations. It may even be considered rude to let your phone ring, depending upon the circumstances.

If you must have your mobile phone nearby during work hours, set it to vibrate so as not to disturb others. Mobile phones should not be used during meetings, dinners, or lunches, or when you are supposed to be performing your work duties. If your phone is set to vibrate, place it somewhere where the vibration will not disturb others. For instance, if the mobile phone is on a desk surface, the vibration could cause it to bounce against the surface and annoy those nearby.

Speakerphones are convenient when multiple people must participate in a teleconference. However, several participants speaking at once during a teleconference will confuse those listening in. It is often difficult to maintain order when people are not visibly present. Establish clear guidelines for participants beforehand so you will be assured of an efficient procedure.

Another convenience of using speakerphones is the hands-free convenience when you are on hold. This allows you to listen for the person for which you are holding while you are able to move around and complete other tasks.

Extreme noises on either end of the line will distort calls and make it difficult to hear anyone who speaks. When using a speakerphone, close your office door or go to a remote area where you will not disturb others. Lower the volume to minimize the effects of people who speak in a loud voice and may be overheard. Never divulge personal or confidential information over a speakerphone, as someone who should not be privy to the conversation might overhear it on your end or on the listener's end. In addition, remember that the listener will be able to hear conversations going on in the area around the telephone and any other noise that originates on your end of the line.

When the person called answers the phone, remove him from the speakerphone unless it is necessary for multiple callers to hear the message.

You will find additional information on mobile phones in Chapter 9, "Adapt to Personalities and Situations."

Be considerate of others when using the telephone.

52.

Do Not Invade Co-Workers' Personal Space

People can be very territorial about their workspace and what they perceive as their possessions and entitlements. This causes them to become defensive when they feel someone has invaded their space or has become embroiled in their personal business. They also do not like it when someone takes what they perceive are their things. It does not matter if the workspace and supplies are company property. When assigned to an individual, she perceives them to be hers.

You must be thoughtful of the rights of others. As you would resent someone going through your personal belongings or prying in your company or personal matters, your co-workers would begrudge your taking over their space, searching through their things, or meddling in their affairs.

Respect your co-workers' rights to their personal work area without intrusion. What you may believe is a good excuse for being in someone's office could be considered an annoyance or even an invasion of privacy. While waiting for a co-worker in his workspace, do not seat yourself in her chair when she is not in her office or place your personal possessions on or in her desk or cabinets. The only time you should place things in another person's office or on her desk, including messages, is when you are asked to do so. Avoid snooping in your co-worker's drawers and cabinets or on her computer or desktop.

Do not presume to make a call on her phone or use her computer without permission. Never attempt to learn someone else's password or access a computer using another's password without permission. This could be considered hacking.

Ask before taking anything from another person's work area, including office supplies. You may believe you are simply borrowing the object, but your co-worker may feel common courtesy or protocol has been breached even if the object technically belongs to the company.

Respect boundaries established for shared spaces, supplies, and equipment. For instance, if you share a desk but each of you has a personal drawer, refrain from opening the other person's drawer. Work around items your co-worker displays on the desk (for example, pictures, a calendar, or a plant). Make an effort to find furnishings acceptable to everyone involved.

Before sending a document to a shared printer, alert co-workers, especially when documents are several pages long. Refill empty paper trays.

Wipe shared phones and other equipment with a sanitizer whenever you have a cold or other illness so as not to infect co-workers. Keep shared areas safe. A person who habitually leaves a cabinet door or file drawer open is creating a hazard for others. He may have to be told in a constructive manner to close all doors and drawers.

Problems occasionally arise when something one person does in a shared space irritates another. Try to resolve differences in a constructive manner. Is your co-worker's plant in an inconvenient spot? Would she mind moving it? Perhaps you could suggest it would thrive near the window. Does your co-worker leave her work scattered across the desk you share? Could you arrange bins or baskets for her to store the work when it is your turn to use the desk? Think of cooperative solutions instead of focusing on your irritation.

Because humans are creatures of habit, a co-worker may feel he is entitled to the same chair in the lunchroom every day. Why not let him sit there?

Personal space around us is also important. According to an individual's culture, you may have to keep a respectable distance while interacting in business and personal situations. Inappropriate touching, which again could vary among cultures, should be avoided. Make it a point to understand the customs of your co-workers so as not to infringe on their rights or seem rude.

Respect the personal spaces of those with whom you work.

53.

Don't Treat the Office as Your Personal Grooming Station

Some people treat the office as their personal grooming station. Although you will want to exhibit a professional appearance, avoid grooming yourself in the workspace, particularly where others can witness it, such as cubicles, open work spaces, and shared offices. Combing hair, spraying perfume, clipping nails, picking teeth, using a lint roller, applying makeup, and tugging clothing into place should be handled in private. If you must attend to a personal grooming emergency, go to the nearest restroom or secluded area.

Maintain a neat, clean appearance, but groom yourself in private.

54.
Keep Smells to a Minimum

Perfume or cologne, hair products and sprays, body washes and sprays, lotions, hand sanitizers, and the like are meant to smell pleasant. To someone who is allergic to those products or who abhors a particular fragrance, however, they are not so pleasant. Dousing yourself with fragrant products that leave a lingering scent long after you have departed is offensive to everyone, not just those with allergies. Apply these products with a light touch.

Foods can leave pleasant or unpleasant odors, depending on how people feel about them. What you might think smells delicious might repel someone else. Avoid bringing foods to work that have a strong odor of any kind or that leave a lingering unpleasant smell.

Candles and air fresheners may counteract unpleasant smells, but be sure they do not create a worse effect on individuals who have allergies.

Workers exhibiting poor hygiene create an unpleasant environment and make co-workers uncomfortable. From body odors and general uncleanliness to an unkempt appearance and inappropriate clothing, employees who are oblivious to their offensive grooming habits cause their co-workers to avoid them. Use good grooming and oral hygiene to avoid offensive, unpleasant body odors. Shower daily, wash your hair, and use deodorant and mouthwash. If you find your co-workers avoiding you, check your personal hygiene and grooming.

If you are in the position of having to advise someone of their poor hygiene practices, assume he is unaware of offending others. Show empathy. Take him aside to a private area to discuss an awkward, embarrassing problem. It is better to address the problem as soon as possible with honesty and empathy. Postponing this difficult conversation will not make the problem go away. Hinting about the problem without specifically stating it rarely works.

Products and supplies used in the completion of your work may emit odors and fumes that require ventilation. Take proper precautions when working with toxic products and wear all required safety clothing and equipment.

Smells, even ones that are pleasant to you, may bother those with whom you work.

55.

Send Professional Emails

Company emails are business documents and should be treated as such whenever you are composing them. Just because email is a quick, easy way to correspond does not mean it should be treated casually. Polished emails send a message that you are a professional. Write them with the same care as you would a letter.

Typical business emails contain informative facts, requests for information or assistance, meeting details, and similar work-related items required to conduct business and complete tasks. Negative news and confidential information should not be delivered via email.

Compose email messages with your reader in mind. Is the message easy to understand? Will the reader be familiar with the words you use? Words geared to a wide audience and educational level will be most effective. If your reader does not understand your words, the message will be lost. Did you give complete information so the receiver will know what to do when she reads the email? Use business language and an acceptable format complete with proper salutation and a closing line identifying the sender.

An appropriate subject line will inform the email recipient of the nature of the message. Keep the subject title short and be precise so the reader can easily identify the contents. This will aid in prioritizing. If you are responding to an email but it is not the same subject, change the subject line to reflect the new topic.

Because emails are informal, take care that the tone of the message is not so friendly as to seem unprofessional or inappropriate. Write clearly using as few words as possible while giving complete details. Spell words in full unless a shortened form of a word is acceptable for business purposes. Avoid odd or unusual fonts, emoticons, and pictures, as these distract from your message. Typing in all capitals is the equivalent of yelling and is considered aggressive.

Keep emails to a manageable length by getting right to the point. If you have a lot to say, send a letter, not a verbose email. These days, people are inundated by emails and do not have time to sort through extensive messages to get the information they need. Also remember that lengthy attachments, pictures, and charts generally require a long time to download, and many people resent wasting time waiting for an email attachment to open. Many people refuse to open attachments from unknown sources because of viruses. In addition, if the recipient does not have the correct software, she may not be able to open the attachment.

Mark high-priority items as needed, but only flag emails with priority markings when they are urgent. Otherwise, people will realize you are falsely vying for their attention and will begin to ignore your emails.

Any information you send via company email can be intercepted and read by your employer and possibly others. This should encourage you to write only positive emails about your company, supervisors, co-workers, and customers. Think before sending emails that might have an adverse effect on your career.

Unopened, unresolved business email messages can lead to missing information and create difficulties for you and your company. Unanswered emails may result in lost money, time, and customers, and could damage your reputation. Check emails regularly and respond in a timely manner. Procrastinating will cause a buildup of emails, but you will eventually have to address those of a business nature. Stress levels may also increase as worry over accumulating emails increases. Strive to empty your email inbox daily or at least keep emails to a minimum. Prioritize large volumes of emails.

When time is limited, check the subject lines of emails to determine the most efficient method of handling messages. Email messages that pose a problem that cannot be immediately addressed should be answered with a follow-up email. Let the sender know you received the message and will resolve the issue as soon as possible. Supply a timeline if you can. Sometimes, however, you will not be able to oblige the sender. In that case, you must let him know as soon as possible.

Never read other people's emails or access their email accounts without permission. To do so is an inexcusable violation of privacy. Do not improperly search for another person's passcodes.

On a similar note, email accounts can be hacked. Never send confidential information via email. Assume anyone can access your email account and take precautions to protect yourself. Compose multiple passcodes for your various email accounts. Avoid using birthdays and common words. A combination of nonsensical letters and numbers will make it difficult for others to access your account. Change passcodes often.

Think twice before sending jokes and other social emails. It is annoying to have to delete unwanted emails and a waste of time. It may also be against company policies to send anything that is not business related.

Junk emails clog up email mailboxes and cause the recipient irritation and time. It also causes frustration and anger. Some junk email may even be illegal to send. Never send gossip via email. It could be traced to you, and gossip is frowned upon by management.

Do not copy people on emails if the message does not pertain to them. Be careful when replying to emails. If you are responding to an email thread, trim the message so the recipients do not have to read every message to get to the latest one. If anyone on the original email list does not need the information, be considerate and do not send it to him. People receive enough emails they have to read and answer without being bombarded with messages they do not need.

Double-check before clicking send so you do not send a message by mistake. It may cost you your job. If you accidentally send an unprofessional or confidential email to the wrong person, do whatever you can to rectify the mistake and minimize the damage it will cause. Contact those affected and apologize.

Here is a summary of email guidelines:

- Compose emails using professional language and proper grammar and punctuation.
- Use common fonts. Do not mix various fonts and colors.
- Use appropriate, informative subject lines.
- Be selective when flagging messages for priority.
- Never send sensitive information or bad news via email.
- Avoid using slang, shortened versions of words, emoticons, and all caps.
- Use spellcheck and proofread your emails before clicking send.
- Use appropriate salutations and closings.
- Properly identify yourself and, when appropriate, your company.
- Choose strong passcodes to protect your email accounts.
- Avoid sending jokes and unwanted junk mail.
- Never access anyone's email account without his permission.
- Check company emails regularly.

Treat emails as proper business documents. Use common courtesy when sending emails.

56.
Ditch Annoying Habits

Annoying habits can drive people mad and create a taxing workplace situation. Although people need to be tolerant of idiosyncrasies, it is not fair to subject them to annoying, pointless irritants.

Daily nuisances can build to the degree an individual is bothered enough to complain to a supervisor or to evade the offender. If aggravated enough, she may be driven to confront the offender in a hostile manner.

You may feel justified in displaying your quirky mannerisms, but remember you are sharing space with other people who have the right to an annoyance-free, stress-free workplace. If you have been warned of a habit that irritates others, rid yourself of the habit.

Avoid these habits that tend to annoy others:

- Chewing or cracking gum
- Making noises while eating
- Smacking lips
- Burping
- Slurping

- Constant throat clearing
- Cracking knuckles
- Tapping fingers or feet
- Clicking pens
- Similar noisy habits

Texting while others are working or during meetings and meals has become a problem. It is rude to send and check texts whenever your attention should be on the people you are with and your work. It is also impolite to ignore a speaker in other ways such as by reading or writing something that has nothing to do with the meeting or business situation.

Even what you consider a pleasant habit can be bothersome to others, such as singing, humming, or talking to yourself. Many people require silence to concentrate on their work and to assist customers and visitors.

Telling a co-worker or supervisor she has an annoying habit is tricky. Tact and understanding will help.

Be aware of and avoid habits that annoy others.

57.
Do Not Be a Backstabber

Some people pretend to be a friend and speak kindly to a person's face but turn around and say things about her behind her back. Such betrayals are not only deceitful but also hurtful. The person who betrays is untrustworthy. She rarely contains her remarks to one or two people but rather talks about anyone. Believe she will talk about you given the opportunity.

Be vigilant of anything you say about other people that may cause complications for you or hurt that person's feelings or reputation in any way. Otherwise, you may be perceived as a backstabber.

Another form of backstabbing is taking undue credit from someone. Do not offer to help someone and then turn around and take credit for doing the job or tell everyone that the person you offered to help could not do the job himself so you had to do it. Claiming someone else's idea as your own is a lie and is immoral. This includes adapting someone else's idea and taking full credit.

If you cannot speak kindly, refrain from speaking.

6

BUILD POSITIVE
RELATIONSHIPS

For people to get along at work, each person must appreciate the other. Appreciation promotes respect and amicability. Cultures, beliefs, principles, and attitudes combine to make people unique and, as such, valued. Recognize in a positive way the differences people bring to the workplace and what you can learn from everyone around you. Through tolerance and understanding, employees create harmony in a diverse workplace.

Exhibiting good manners, proper etiquette, and positive personal traits will demonstrate a high regard for all people. Consider how your actions affect others in the workplace. Be supportive by making your actions kind and considerate.

58.
Avoid Arguments

It is inevitable that people will disagree in work situations just as they disagree in other areas of their lives. However, it is one thing to disagree and quite another to let disagreements escalate into bickering or full-scale arguments. Some arguments turn ruthless and so do the participants. Who wins in such a dispute? Those embroiled in the quarrel may each feel they are winners because of having had their say or standing their ground, but there are generally no big winners in vehement arguments. More than likely all parties will lose in some way. Do your part to disagree in a civilized manner and minimize quarrels.

Address everyone with courtesy. No one likes to be treated rudely or to be made to feel incompetent or worthless. Monitor what you say and do at all times. It only takes one misstep to hurt a co-worker's feelings, alienate a customer, or ruin a relationship with a supervisor. You may have treated a person with courtesy for years, but the one time you do not will be the time she will remember.

Hostility in any form places co-workers in no-win situations. During confrontations, stay calm and control your emotions and temper. Anger does nothing to help the situation. A non-threatening, temperate approach with supportive language composed of courteous, kind words will assure the other person you are not looking to argue or fight.

Some people have bad manners and are short-tempered. They complain about everything and go out of their way to look for an argument. If you know a dispute will be inevitable every time you encounter a certain person, do what you can to avoid her and stay clear of the threat. Is it absolutely necessary that you see or talk with her? Must you be involved in the situation with her or can someone else handle the affair? Could you delay an encounter with her until both of you have had a chance to settle down? Could you ask an indifferent third party to oversee the situation so it does not get out of control? Could a trusted friend give you pointers on how to get along during those difficult encounters? If it is impossible to avoid the negative co-worker, ignore her by reminding yourself she is not worth your getting upset.

When a co-worker offends you, try not to overreact to the offense. Look at the whole picture before making a judgment. Could you have misread the action? Is it a minor annoyance or major infraction? Is it worth a confrontation or would it be best to ignore the offense? Do you see any way to resolve the issue amicably? Anticipate the consequences of any action you plan to take and abort that act if you believe it will escalate the confrontation. Do your best to avoid arguments, disputes, and disrespectful behaviors that create a hostile environment.

What if someone pushes you to the point you want to push back? A decision to challenge a hostile worker should not be taken lightly. You may be placing yourself in harm's way or your temper may cause harm to the other person. Use a courteous, practical manner, focusing on the behavior rather than the individual to minimize fault-finding. Explain how you feel by using "I" statements. Stick to the particulars without going overboard on the details. Simple language and explanations generally work best. Ask questions meant to learn facts, not to interrogate the person on his motives.

Distance yourself from problematic, malicious, and manipulative co-workers. They are not worth risking your reputation or career. Issues with a particularly difficult or abusive co-worker should be discussed with your supervisor or other professional who can help you arrive at viable options for dealing with the person. Actions that violate your rights or cause harm should be reported immediately to the proper company personnel or authorities.

Remember these tips:

- Watch your tone.
- Express sincerity.
- Speak with kindness.
- Show understanding.
- Convey a polite attitude.
- Value every person.
- Take a step back.
- Look for an amicable resolution.
- Avoid argumentative people.
- Avoid confrontations.

Build positive relationships based on courtesy and respect for everyone.

59.
Stay Home When You Are Sick

Although you will want to have good attendance at work, you should not go if you are sick, especially if your illness could infect others. While some people report in sick when they are not, others who are sick drag themselves to work when they have no business being there. These latter workers act as if the place could not operate without them.

You may feel your work will suffer if you take off a day, but consider the complications associated with going to work ill. You may have difficulty performing your duties satisfactorily. You may be prone to making mistakes or overlooking important details. If you operate equipment, you may be a danger to yourself and others when you are not physically healthy and mentally prepared. Medications prescribed for your illness could further complicate the issue by making you drowsy and, therefore, error and accident prone.

Your patience may suffer when you are ill and cause you to respond to a co-worker or customer with a curt remark or worse. Perhaps you will seem unfriendly or unaccommodating to your customers, thus costing the company a good customer's future business. Your illness may even leave you physically unable to give customers the stellar service they deserve. In addition, not taking the time to rest and recuperate could have adverse effects on your health. Pushing yourself may cause the illness to linger or worsen or to develop into a more serious medical condition.

Going to work sick may cost your employer additional time and money if you infect others and they then miss work for their own recovery. Sick employees risk exposing co-workers, customers, and anyone else with whom they come into contact. They contaminate the office and the equipment they operate with their germs, spreading their sickness.

When you feel an illness coming on, stay away from others to the extent you can. Cover your mouth when you sneeze or cough and avoid shaking hands.

If your company has a policy for sick days and sick leave, follow the proper procedures. For instance, call and report in sick for the day and bring a doctor's excuse if required. Prepare for longer sick leaves in advance if possible.

Never abuse sick policies. Calling in sick when you are not ill is unethical.

Practice preventative measures to stay healthy and take precautions to avoid getting sick by doing these things:

▪ Frequently wash your hands and use hand sanitizers.

▪ Do not touch public surfaces and then touch your face.

▪ Disinfect any equipment and tools you share.

▪ Spray areas where sick people have been.

▪ Keep eating surfaces clean to prevent food-borne illnesses. Clean food and drink spills.

▪ Get proper rest.

▪ Eat healthy foods.

▪ Avoid people who are sick.

▪ Consult your doctor or medical professional.

To avoid infecting others, stay home when you are sick.

60.

Be Tolerant of Others' Beliefs and Cultural Differences

In a multicultural country and a global economy, people of all cultures will likely be connected to each other. It is important to find ways to make these connections positive ones. Begin by maintaining a tolerant attitude. All workers in a global economy may be in a position to connect with people from multiple cultures. Take advantage of this exceptional learning opportunity.

Abolish preconceived ideas, stereotypical thinking, and prejudices. Bias causes us to interpret things according to how we "see" them in our minds—and not always for the better. For instance, one person might see a multicultural workforce as a positive situation where everyone is equal and new ideas will flourish, while another person may see that same diverse workforce as a negative.

People have a wide range of beliefs stemming from their backgrounds, cultures, personalities, and life experiences. Not everyone will think and act as you believe they should. Accept each person as an individual who has the right to express his individuality. Show a willingness to allow people to be themselves without discriminating against them or imposing your belief system on them. Censure your actions and speech when you are in the company of people from other cultures so as not to insult or intimidate them. Do not talk negatively about a particular culture or its people.

Acknowledge the value in diversity by welcoming different viewpoints. Cultivate friendships with people from diverse cultures to learn about life in other parts of the world. Remember, differences are not wrong or negative. They are just differences. If you work on a regular basis with people of a certain culture, take the time to learn something about that culture.

Promote ethnic diversity by encouraging co-workers who have backgrounds different from yours to tell you about their cultures. Be attentive and listen with interest to their personal experiences. What is distinctive about their lives? What are the highlights of their countries? Have you discovered something interesting or unusual that you did not already know? What are their national holidays and religious customs? What are their favorite traditions? You may find it a fun and rewarding experience to learn how people in other parts of the world celebrate. Could you incorporate any of these traditions into the company holiday party or decorating scheme? What are their favorite foods? Could you plan a multicultural luncheon at work? How about exchanging recipes? Can you learn a co-worker's language or even a few key phrases? Take a turn and share your cultural experiences, too. Are their similarities?

In addition to the personal and social aspects of other cultures, you can learn new business practices and ways of doing a job. Draw on the unique talents and contributions of your multinational co-workers. What are their strengths? How do they go about solving problems? How do they perform their tasks? Did they learn to do things differently in their country? Can you learn novel ways of doing your job by noting how these co-workers perform? Having input from a number of sources gives you options.

Because cultural expectations and attitudes are so varied, individuals may cause offense or commit an indiscretion without realizing it. Greetings, gestures, handshakes, language, foods, personal space, dress, beliefs, habits, and so forth vary among cultures. You might do something the way you have always done it but end up insulting someone because you are unaware of how things are said or done in his culture. For instance, a gesture that means "okay" in your country may be an obscene gesture in another country. A willingness to learn about others will prevent you from offending them unintentionally.

There are many cultural considerations in addition to gestures, including attitudes and other nonverbal communications like expressions and posture. Political and religious views can be formidable topics. Another major consideration for business professionals is a country's dress code. Men may be required to wear suits and ties in some countries while doing business. Women may be required to wear dresses instead of pants. The best advice is to dress conservatively. If in doubt as to what to wear, research proper dress for the country to which you are traveling for business. Even the manner in which business meals and meetings are conducted varies from country to country.

If you plan to travel to a foreign country on business, learn about the customs and philosophies of that country. Failure to do so could result in embarrassing errors, the consequences of which could be lost relationships and commerce.

Apologize when you make a mistake. Let the person know it was not deliberate and you would like to learn the proper way to handle the situation in the future.

Learn about different cultures and value diversity.

61.

Be Persuasive (When Necessary)

All people are persuasive to some degree. We are always selling ourselves through our skills and point of view, attempting to convince others we are resourceful and are correct in our thinking. We persuade co-workers to buy into our ideas and customers to buy our products. We sell our boss on the fact that we are competent, productive employees and worth our paychecks. We persuade ourselves to work hard.

Using persuasion to improve a situation or to benefit an individual or a company is a positive thing. When laced with malicious intent, however, persuasion has a detrimental effect. For example, persuasion intended to encourage someone to do something that might harm him or someone else or create difficulties for him is wrong and should be stopped. Never coerce anyone.

You might have to persuade someone to do something he does not want to do but is required to do. For example, he may procrastinate when he should be computing a year's worth of figures for a sales report. How do you keep him from missing a deadline? Or you may have to persuade him to work on a team in another division doing a task he normally does not do. How do you persuade him without turning the situation into an argument or having him resent you or his new team members?

Presenting the facts to an individual in a way that clearly shows how he will benefit by doing as you say is a good way to start the persuasive conversation. Back up your claim with valid facts and figures. The right endorsements and recommendations can also be convincing.

Persuasive techniques you can use include the following:

- Speak of the benefits to the other person.
- Use a friendly, sincere tone.
- Establish trust. Never lie to obtain your desired results.
- Use persuasive language.
- Appeal with facts and logic.
- Provide evidence to support your facts.
- Link your statements to something the other person can relate to or already believes.
- Provide testimonials or expert opinions if available.
- Create the desire for an agreement.
- Express the facts in easy-to-understand language.
- Address the other person's concerns in a factual manner.
- Do not lecture.
- Repeat the facts.
- Demonstrate the validity of your position.
- Make sure instructions are well-defined.
- Do not command or demand.

Use persuasion to your benefit as long as it adds value to the other person.

62.

Acknowledge Differences and Recognize Unique Qualities

Differences among people are apparent in lots of ways—age, race, religion, gender, nationality, abilities, and more. We also have physical differences such as height, weight, appearance, complexion, and strength. We have varied backgrounds—education, socioeconomics, family, work histories, culture, and more.

Individuals are unique in their combination of these qualities. Understanding and valuing this uniqueness will have a significant impact on how we respond to others. Treat people not as different, but as distinctive. Keep in mind that a person does not necessarily represent a particular group and you should not generalize. For example, do not assume all women have the same capabilities, thoughts, feelings, etc., or that all young people act immature or that older people are slow. Such generalities promote prejudices that foster injustice and discrimination.

Prejudice of any kind leads to personal judgments based on preconceived ideas, incomplete information, or distorted thinking. These biases are destructive to the person carrying them as well as anyone on whom he projects those beliefs. Practice tolerance and acceptance with an open-minded attitude.

People in a workplace do not all have to be alike and think the same thoughts to have a harmonious environment. In fact, variety makes the workplace interesting by stimulating fascinating conversations and situations. Value the differences among your co-workers and customers.

Although you and your co-workers, supervisor, and customers may be different in many ways, you will probably have some commonalities. Use these shared traits to strengthen friendships. Discussing sports, politics, family life, hobbies, music, entertainment, and fashion are just some of the many ways you might connect with others.

Appreciate the uniqueness of individuals. Become totally inclusive in connecting with people.

63.
Be Observant

You can learn a lot by being mindful of what is going on around you. Start by paying attention to those with whom you work. What is important to them? What annoys them? What do they do on a regular basis? What kind of attitudes do they have? What verbal and nonverbal clues do they project?

Observe how people behave and interact in your workplace. How do co-workers relate to each other? Are they thoughtful and respectful or rude and overbearing? How do subordinates relate to the supervisor and how does he relate to them? What can you learn from these behaviors? What you discover can be helpful whether the behaviors are negative or positive. You can learn how to act or how not to act.

Pay attention to workplace chats and discussions. How do co-workers speak to each other, to supervisors, and to customers? Listen to their vocabulary and the meaning they attach to specific words. What is their tone? How does each person react to what is being said to him? How do people listen to each other? Are they attentive or inattentive? How do they react to what is said to them?

Notice how your co-workers, supervisor, and customers interact with you. Do you feel positive about your experiences with them? Does anything particularly positive or negative stand out? This may give you clues as to how you are perceived by them and the way you connect with them.

How do you, in turn, relate to everyone else? Pay attention to your own behavior to determine if you should make changes in your attitude or conduct. An honest assessment of your connection with others can lead to self-awareness and the opportunity to grow or to change if necessary.

You will want to expand your observations to determine who the successful people are in your company. How do they speak, act, and relate to others? How do the most successful supervisors treat subordinates? Can you model these outstanding co-workers and supervisors? Will their methods work for you?

Turn your observations to the different types of jobs performed in your company. How are the various tasks accomplished? Are they completed in the most efficient way? Can you determine areas for improvement? If so, can you suggest a better way?

Develop a curiosity about your tasks. Pay attention to the details in completing the work. What can you do to improve? Is there anything more you can do to increase your productivity? Notice the quality and quantity of your work and how it measures up to the work of those around you. Does your work meet or exceed your supervisor's and your company's expectations?

When it comes to completing your own tasks, look at what you are doing and ask yourself these questions:

- Am I on the right track, or am I merely going through the motions?
- Am I being as proficient as possible?
- How would someone else do the same job?
- How do my co-workers do their jobs?
- Do co-workers have positive habits I can adopt?
- Do co-workers have habits I believe I should avoid?
- Is my supervisor pleased with my work?
- Do I need to make changes?
- How can I improve?

If you are a supervisor, you will want to pay attention to what is going on with your subordinates. Ask yourself questions about your subordinates such as these:

- Are they productive?
- Is their work accurate?
- Are their skills up to date?
- Do they follow company policies and procedures?
- Do they seem satisfied?
- Do they get along with each other?
- Am I open to their suggestions?
- Do I listen to their concerns?
- Do I address their concerns in a satisfactory manner?

Monitor happenings throughout your company so you are in a position to contribute in the best way possible. Pay attention to the latest trends in your industry, particularly those that could affect you and your company.

Be observant. Know what is going on around you and how it affects you.

64.
Remember Perception

Sometimes seeing is believing; sometimes it is not. How we perceive or view something may be radically different from how another perceives or views it. Even a picture could look different to people who observe it. The subject matter, lighting, coloring, context in which the picture is viewed, and viewer's life experiences could produce contrasting interpretations. Our minds look at something and try to make sense of it based on our individual makeup.

Two people may be exposed to the same situation under similar conditions or may see or hear the same thing but perceive it differently. For instance, two people could witness a crime but give conflicting descriptions of the event and the perpetrator. Each witness will believe he is accurate in what he saw and heard and his interpretation of it. Or two employees could receive the same directive from the boss and interpret it in a different way. One may have thought the boss meant to stop everything and do the job right now and the other might have thought the boss meant finish what you are doing and perform the other task as soon as possible.

People form perceptions of what they hear, see, and believe based on their beliefs, customs, age, education, gender, interests, past history, experiences, preferences, and so on. With so many varied backgrounds and life experiences, it is easy to see how people can have different insights into what they see and hear.

A situation one person may perceive as a major setback might be a minor inconvenience to another. Keep things in perspective. Do not let your imagination create a tragedy out of a small impediment.

Because people put their own spin on things, it follows that their assessments are not always accurate. Their views may be skewed by something in their makeup or belief system. They may be convinced something is true when it is not. They may be able to totally convince themselves they are correct.

It is difficult to change perceptions or even misperceptions because people are so clearly convinced of what they see or hear. They may not even be able to change their perception if proven wrong because their particular background and life experiences may be so ingrained that they cannot adjust their thinking.

Be perceptive about yourself. You may see yourself in a certain way that others do not. For instance, you may feel you are an expert in a certain area, but others may not share your view. Or you might not feel you are an expert and others may believe you are. You may think you are being helpful and concerned, while another person may feel you are a meddler and intrusive.

On the other hand, you are constantly forming opinions yourself, and you may have an incorrect perception of someone else. For instance, if you speak with someone who looks down when he talks, you may have the impression he is lying. However, the truth might be that people in his culture avoid direct eye contact. Or you may think a job candidate who bites her nails is nervous, when in reality it may just be a negative habit and she is not nervous at all.

Seeing is not always believing.

65.
Avoid Loud Talking, Laughing, and Joking

Workplaces should be conducive to conducting business. As such, they should be quiet and accommodating. Employees should be respectful of each other and behave in a professional manner.

Some people cannot concentrate in a noisy environment. Loud talking and laughing are annoying and inappropriate when they interrupt others who are working. Not everyone thinks joking and fooling around are fun, especially when they are trying to work. Be considerate by keeping your voice lowered.

Gathering places like water coolers, vending machines, and copiers tempt people to congregate and socialize. Although you want to be on friendly terms with your co-workers, limit socializing to breaks and lunchtime. Even then, restrict such behavior when it offends or disturbs others who prefer a quieter environment. It is especially important to maintain control of your actions in shared spaces and public areas. Customers who come to your place of business may think your company and its employees are not dependable and responsible if they see people reveling instead of working.

Supervisors take daily actions into consideration when promoting individuals. By remaining professional at all times, you show the supervisor you are a responsible person and can be depended on to do your work.

Conduct yourself in a professional manner at all times in the workplace.

66.
Look for Positives in Negative Behaviors and Situations

Difficulties and complications afflict everyone's life, so it stands to reason you will encounter them in the workplace. An optimistic outlook will help you deal with these difficulties in a constructive manner.

Sometimes we have to make the best of a less-than-ideal situation. Your company may be undergoing remodeling that inconveniences everyone, a modification in organization or restructuring of assets, or other major change. A negative encounter with a customer may threaten to ruin your day. A disagreement with the supervisor or a co-worker could set you on edge. Any time you are in a situation where you have to deal with other people, there is always the possibility of misunderstandings and differences of opinions. What can you learn from the situation?

An error you made could add pressure to your already burdened schedule. Accept that you are human and make mistakes. What can you do to fix it?

You may have lost a big account or even your job. How can you recover the account or find a new source of income? Where can you apply for another job? Start looking for a solution immediately instead of dwelling on what happened.

Any number of things can and do go wrong. Those individuals who have a knack for dealing with unfortunate situations generally have an optimistic outlook. They look for ways to solve problems rather than surrender to them.

If you have trouble being optimistic, surround yourself with co-workers and others who are upbeat and cheerful and who will encourage you.

An optimistic attitude will help you overlook troublesome situations.

67.
Negotiate Win-Win Situations

Working with a variety of individuals and their varied personalities requires give and take from both sides. By negotiating and perhaps compromising, you communicate your willingness to promote a winning workplace. Sometimes it is better to forgo being right if it means too many people, or even your company, will lose.

Faced with a disagreement, you must decide whether to enter into a dispute or relinquish the need to be right and give up the debate. Will you be able to find a way to come to an agreement that will make everyone involved happy? Lose control, and you may never gain the cooperation of others.

Manipulation or trickery will undermine trust and goodwill. Consequently, the relationship will suffer. This is particularly damaging when you must connect on a regular basis with the person you have manipulated.

Often a customer will demand that you resolve his problem in a way that goes against company policy or your better judgment. In such cases, it may be necessary to negotiate a compromise or a concession to maintain the customer's business while still adhering to company policies and procedures.

Here are tips for negotiating:

- Genuinely listen to the other person's point of view.
- Keep an open mind. Do not close your mind to alternatives.
- Express yourself in clear, positive language.
- Have empathy for the other person.
- Use non-threatening statements.
- Avoid tricks and manipulations.
- Look for acceptable trade-offs.
- Seek a solution that benefits everyone.

Be agreeable—compromise.

68.
Be Attentive

Have you ever strolled into a place of business, walked up to the receptionist, and been ignored while you stood there waiting for help? Have you ever walked into a store and had the salespeople scatter in the other direction or been ignored by multiple salespeople who were chatting when they should have been assisting you? Have you had to wait while the salesperson carried on a personal phone call? Have you encountered co-workers who do not return your phone calls or answer your emails, leaving you unable to finish your work while their part of the task was missing? Have you ignored anyone in the same manner?

Knowing how irritating it is to be ignored by others, we should never ignore customers, co-workers, or the supervisor. All it takes is a quick nod or smile to acknowledge someone and let them know you will be with them in a minute.

It is sometimes tempting to tune out a ringing telephone, to continue working on your own tasks when a co-worker needs your assistance, or to ignore a customer who comes to your counter. However, a conscientious worker will do none of these.

It is irritating to be ignored when you know the other person is aware of your presence. Knowing you are being ignored is frustrating enough, but knowing the person is ignoring you because of personal business is even more maddening. Ignoring co-workers can affect work relationships in a negative way. Ignoring customers can seriously damage customer relations. Ignore the boss and it could cost you your job.

Greet people and give them your full attention the moment you are able to do so. When someone approaches you, stop what you are doing and look up and acknowledge him. Sit up straight (or stand), listen carefully, and respond appropriately.

Sometimes you are genuinely busy with another customer or on an important company phone call. If that is the case, at least acknowledge the person waiting with a nod or a wave indicating you will be with him soon. You might also make eye contact and smile. If possible, say, "I will be with you as soon as I finish with this customer." When you do attend to him, apologize for the delay and do what you can for him.

If a co-worker needs your attention, acknowledge him. Find out what he needs and provide it. If you are unable to help at that time, say so. If you can help at another time, let him know.

Do not ignore people. Acknowledge them with a nod, smile, or other greeting.

69.

Practice Patience

When you encounter a trying person or situation, strive to think of it as a lesson in learning patience…and then learn the lesson. Sometimes having a little patience makes a big difference in how a situation or our interactions with others turn out.

Being patient with others may give you the leverage you need to resolve a situation and it may even gain you allies. You may be able to defuse a volatile situation or encourage someone who needs it. You might be able to make a sale to that customer who is having trouble making up his mind about a product. Your co-worker might benefit from your patient training on how to do his job.

You may want to hurry along the project, but a little patience may be a better plan. Hurrying can result in mistakes or omissions. You will want to work efficiently but carefully enough to be accurate. Patience allows for careful preparation that can help you do your job in a more proficient manner.

It may seem like a good idea to push co-workers or subordinates to get more done, but will that be productive and efficient in the long run? What if they make mistakes or stress over the pressure? You could lose valuable employees.

Make adjustments in your approach that will give you the patience needed to unlock solutions, help you deal with various personalities, ignore minor irritations, and tolerate inconveniences.

Be patient with yourself and others.

PART III

INTERACTING WITH CUSTOMERS, CHIEFS, AND CO-WORKERS

7

ENGAGE SUCCESSFULLY WITH CO-WORKERS AND CUSTOMERS

To engage successfully with co-workers, you will want to build positive relationships. Be friendly, but not overly friendly. Exhibit self-control at all times. Maintain a businesslike demeanor while at work and when attending company social functions, whether it is a picnic, sporting event, or holiday party.

A team-player attitude will help you succeed on the job, as teams can complete work faster and often more resourcefully than individuals. Team players work with the team to solve problems creatively, invent new products and processes, and come up with great ideas.

Make the best use of your talents and help others to do the same. Always strive to better yourself and increase your productivity and efficiency.

70.
Be Wary of Socializing

You will spend a lot of time in the workplace and will want to make friends. Socializing at work is a way to connect with co-workers, supervisors, and customers. It is a good way to discover something you like about others and build camaraderie. It provides an opportunity to meet new people or reconnect with those you rarely see.

However, socializing whenever you are supposed to be working is frowned upon in most companies if it interferes with productivity. You are paid to work, not to hang around and waste time.

It is understandable that you will need to take breaks to keep yourself refreshed. However, wasting valuable work time goofing off throughout the day is unacceptable. As addressed in tip 65, "Avoid Loud Talking, Laughing, and Joking," breaks and lunch are the optimum times for socializing with co-workers during business hours.

You may have an opportunity to attend company functions ranging from lunches to major events. The manner in which you dress and act will be determined by the occasion. In all instances, though, you will want to dress so people will take you seriously and to conduct yourself appropriately.

Different etiquette rules apply when you are socializing for business as opposed to socializing with friends and relatives. You must dress tastefully and in a fitting manner and act professionally. Avoid objectionable clothing, swearing, unsuitable humor, and obnoxious or tasteless behavior. Where your friends will be forgiving of a transgression, a supervisor, co-worker, or customer may not.

Keep the company's image in mind when dressing for an event. Use discernment and good judgment even for informal affairs. Ask yourself how you will feel interacting with the supervisor dressed in the outfit you have chosen to wear. The same thing applies if you are dressing for a formal occasion or anything in between. Wearing inappropriate clothing sends the wrong message.

While socializing with co-workers or entertaining business guests, steer clear of hot-button topics, insensitive humor, loud discussions, and disagreements so as not to offend anyone. If drinking is appropriate, do so in moderation. Mind your manners and use proper table etiquette.

The annual company holiday party or a conference event can have a negative effect on a career when employees have too good of a time. Individuals who drink to excess, stagger around, talk too loud, tell inappropriate jokes, or divulge too much personal information risk their jobs, future promotions, and even their careers.

If you are a guest at a company meal or function, avoid the aforementioned bad behavior. In addition, take clues from your host to determine what to order and the course of the conversation. Hosts should pay for business guests' meals. These suggestions also apply when you are the one entertaining business guests.

In selecting a restaurant for a business meal, consider the following:

■ A location that is convenient for your guest

■ Good food and service

■ Appropriate amount to spend

■ Ambiance and privacy conducive to talking business

For large-scale events such as conventions, you will be exposed to a wider group of people, perhaps including customers and business associates. They will undoubtedly view improper behavior in a damaging light and get a negative impression of you. Be aware of how your actions may contribute to the erosion of your professional image, the termination of your career aspirations, and the downfall of you or your company. Your reputation is priceless. Maintain self-control in public at all times.

The boss is always the boss, whether you are at work or at a social function. Be respectful. Do not assume you are buddies and cross the line. You can get to know each other on a more personal basis, but do not do or say something you might regret. In addition, the boss may be eyeing you for a promotion, which you would not want to jeopardize.

Before dating someone in your workplace, check the company policy. Some companies prohibit dating among co-workers because it can cause a number of disagreeable problems. A boss and subordinate who date may create even more concerns.

Just as too much socializing is detrimental, not interacting socially with co-workers can also be a mistake. Co-workers may come to see you as unfriendly or standoffish. They may even take it as a personal affront and resent you. Spend some time talking with co-workers at lunch and on breaks. Share knowledge, company communications and procedures, and interests. Take time to acclimate new workers and befriend them. On the other hand, do not disrupt colleagues' work or let their socializing interfere with your job.

Be friendly but businesslike with customers. For instance, you may want to get to know their likes and dislikes with regard to the products and services you can provide for them. Consult your company's policy with regard to receiving gifts from customers or providing them with gifts and amenities.

Never let customers see you goofing off with co-workers during business hours. At the approach of a customer, immediately stop socializing and attend to his needs.

Maintain self-respect while socializing in the workplace and during company functions.

71.
Be Productive

To be productive, fully commit to getting the job done as soon as possible. Get started and do not stop until finished. Manage circumstances that might derail your efforts.

Follow these tips to become more productive:

- Take care of your health.
- Stay organized throughout the day.
- Block off time to do your work.
- Make a to-do list and prioritize items.
- Use your high-energy periods for difficult tasks.
- Break tasks into smaller increments.
- Do something—anything—to start the task.
- Establish a set time for checking and answering emails.
- Establish a set time to return phone calls.
- Focus on one task at a time.
- Minimize distractions.
- Establish deadlines for projects.
- Keep all relevant contact information in a centralized place.
- Take breaks regularly and if possible exercise.
- Make sure you have the proper equipment and that it is in working order.

Apathy can occur when a job is no longer satisfying. If you find yourself becoming apathetic toward your job, you will not be very productive. Do not just go through the motions day after day. Look for ways to make your job interesting. Take pride in your work and the contributions you are making to your company.

It is easy to procrastinate for a number of reasons such as you are overwhelmed, have no idea how to do the job, are tired or hungry, are mentally or physically exhausted, or are ill. The list goes on and on.

The problem with procrastination is that it has its own rewards. It is way too easy not to do something because of all the aforementioned reasons. Although there are lots of ways to procrastinate, the productive person will find that most of them are not compelling enough for her to shirk the responsibility of getting the job done.

If you are a procrastinator, challenge your reasons for procrastinating. Whenever you come up with an excuse to put something off, ask yourself if it is legitimate or if you are sabotaging yourself for no good purpose.

Look over the following examples of reasons for procrastinating and tips for overcoming them:

- **You work well under pressure.** Ask yourself how working under pressure makes you feel. Are you truly enthused about doing the job or are you stressed? Do you get anxious and tired? Being honest with yourself may make you change your mind and stop using that excuse.

- **You are not clear on how to proceed with the task.** Ask for clarification or an example you can follow. Restate what you believe are the directions and ask if you are correct. Create a sample of the task and ask if it is accurate.

- **You believe the job is too difficult.** Break it down into smaller parts. Tell yourself you can do that one part of the job. If you are still having difficulty, determine if you need more instructions or assistance in carrying out the task. Can someone help you or at least better explain the job to you?

- **You feel the task you are doing is boring.** Find a way to make it more pleasant. Can you listen to music while you work? Can you streamline the process? Can you eliminate any part of it that is unnecessary?

- **You do not have the proper skills to complete the job.** Let your supervisor know. Ask if you can be properly trained or if someone who is suitably trained can do the job.

- **You are lazy.** Shape up and get busy. When you are hired to do a job, make up your mind to do it.

There are many reasons people procrastinate. If you can pinpoint the reason you procrastinate, you will be able to address the problem and seek ways to eliminate it. Once you get started, you may find the job is not as difficult or unpleasant as you have built it up to be in your mind.

If you procrastinate for no good reason, you may have to talk yourself out of it. If you think that a task is daunting, unpleasant, or unimportant, convince yourself that doing it will be worthwhile. What do you have to gain? Will it advance your career? Will your boss be happy? Will you be relieved? If nothing else, you can convince yourself it will feel great to have the task completed and behind you.

Procrastinators often get sidetracked. If you get off course, you will have to adjust your behavior and get back on course. Ask what you can do right now to tackle the task at hand. Decide on a plan and carry it out. Forcing yourself to do a task you have been putting off will prove you are a productive person. Then, the next time you are faced with a similar task, you will know you can do it. That may make it easier to get going and to complete the job. You may even discover the task was not as difficult as you had imagined.

You may have to face the fact that the job you have been assigned is not easy or fun, but it needs to be done. Make the best of the situation. Take the first step and then another and another. Sometimes we have to do things we do not want to do.

Give yourself a reward when you complete something you have been putting off. Often procrastinating seems more rewarding than finishing the job. Turn the tables and make finishing the job more rewarding than the procrastination.

Other ways you might break the procrastination habit include these:

- Develop a routine for working on unpleasant tasks.
- Work on a task for five or 10 minutes (set a timer).
- Break down big projects into smaller ones.
- Ask a colleague for help when you are overwhelmed.
- Commit to obtaining results.
- Talk yourself into doing the job.
- Make procrastination worse than actually doing the job.
- Temporarily eliminate access to social media, the Internet, email, phones, and other distractions.
- Find a colleague who is willing to nudge you when you need it.

Find a way to develop inner satisfaction and pride. As you break procrastination habits, congratulate yourself on the achievement.

Putting things off will create problems. Getting things done provides a solution. Commit to getting things done for the sake of your career, job, and company.

72.

Be a Team Player

Companies use teams to complete vital projects as well as routine work. Teams ease the burden on an individual who would have had to accomplish the work alone. Team members working together generally achieve more than an individual because of their collective energy, ideas, and skills. Different team members can be utilized according to their strengths to help each other complete the work faster and more efficiently.

A reliable team player has a strong commitment to the team, makes an effort to connect with and collaborate with everyone, and takes an active role in the team's mission. She understands the team's objectives and her part of the project, gets the job done, does her fair share and beyond, and meets her commitments on deadline. She then follows through to make sure the job is done satisfactorily.

An invaluable skill for a reliable team player is to be an active participant in discussions. Begin by being a good listener. When you are part of a team, be supportive. Listen with an open mind to what team members have to say. Listen for hidden meanings.

When it is your turn to contribute, express your ideas clearly but courteously so others understand your position. Be direct and honest in your assessment of the situation and possible solutions. Convince team members with valid facts. Allow time for feedback from other team members. Accept criticism by not reacting defensively, but instead seeing it as a chance to learn.

Consider all proposed viewpoints and ideas before making a judgment about them or evaluating their merit. Clarify recommendations and other team members' opinions of them so you have an accurate assessment. After having weighed all facts, give your impression of the ideas that team members have contributed. If you do not agree with members about certain points, express your concerns in a positive manner. You do not want to engage in a heated debate, although you can certainly disagree over issues. It does not serve the team for you to go along with everyone else if you believe you have a valid reason for rejecting an idea.

All team members should be involved in all discussions and other means of communication involving the team. Excluding someone undermines the team effort. The information discussed should be kept private among team members.

When the division of duties has been decided, each team member must have a clear picture of what she is to do, to whom she reports, the deadline, and how her individual assignment fits into the big picture of what the team is trying to accomplish. Assist team members who need help, but do not do their work or micromanage them.

Refrain from drawing your own conclusions and trying to implement them. As a group, the team should decide on the best course of action, whether based on your or another team member's ideas. All team members should discuss strategies and solutions and have a say in the team's decision before it is implemented. Everyone may not be in agreement. In cases of dissent, the majority generally rules.

When you come to team meetings, be prepared. Have all files, paperwork, and research you will need completed ahead of time. Be an engaged member by contributing ideas, entering discussions, volunteering for assignments, and assisting others.

Another way to be a successful team player is to be willing to delegate when you are in a leadership position. Many people find it difficult to let go of a project or delegate responsibilities, but if it is in the best interests of co-workers and the company, delegation is the way to go. Keep the good of the team and the company in mind. People like to be empowered and do worthwhile tasks. They often do outstanding work when unrestrained. Give them a chance to show what they can do. Be a leader, but do not boss your co-workers.

Recognize the team's success, even if you only say "Good job!" at the conclusion of the assignment.

Express your team-player attitude by doing the following:

- Build team unity.
- Compromise.
- Be on time for team meetings.
- Listen to all points.
- Reiterate key points.
- Contribute ideas and give your impression of others' ideas.
- Brainstorm ideas with other team members.
- Share your expertise.
- Challenge yourself.
- Help choose a plan of action.
- Volunteer to carry out ideas.
- Get along; be considerate.
- Do your share of the work and more.
- Be a creative, independent thinker.
- Provide feedback.
- Ask for feedback.
- Commit to creating results.
- Tap into other team members' strengths.
- Stay organized throughout the team project.
- Consistently follow through.

Be a cooperative, active team member.

73.
Use Intuition to Sense When There Is a Problem

Have you ever said, "I should have gone with my first instinct?" Often our intuition shows us a way or gives us a nugget of enlightenment that leads to the resolution of a problem, a great idea, or a better way of doing something.

We use intuition when we instinctively know or sense something even when we have no real proof of it. Intuition encompasses our personal thoughts, feelings, and life experiences. It is not necessarily for taking risks, but rather used as an aid in helping us consider the facts in a new light. It allows us to anticipate situations and problems and then rely on what we feel will work, which may or may not be supported by solid evidence.

Sometimes answers are found through an intuitive understanding of a situation or problem. You may have a feeling or a sense you should act in a certain way or do something in a specific way. Often the instincts that guide us provide the correct choice.

As your judgment on the job improves, your intuition may also sharpen, placing you in a better position to make correct judgments.

Look for answers outside the norm by using judgment and inner awareness.

74.
Use Your Talents

We all have a certain talent or special innate ability that allows us to do something well. Some people have multiple innate abilities.

What if you are not sure where your talent lies? Take an aptitude test. Ask your friends and colleagues what they think your talent is. Ask your supervisor or human resource administrator.

Our talents give us a unique way of looking at or doing things. You could have a talent like singing or playing a sport. Your talent could be the compassion you show people who are starving or otherwise burdened. Natural leaders have a talent to manage people. Innovators are naturally creative and see things in a way that most of us do not. Many salespeople have a way of persuading their customers to buy their products and services.

You can take natural talent further by developing it. For instance, if you are a natural at speaking, you could join a speaking organization or take a speech course to learn techniques to further develop that talent. If you are a born leader, you could take management courses to become an outstanding leader. A natural salesperson might attend a sales convention and listen to presentations by super salespeople.

Practicing your talent will increase your ability. Many talented athletes spend hours and hours practicing.

Perhaps you were hired because of your particular talents and the company is counting on you. Do you put your talent to best use? You could talk to co-workers and supervisors who have a similar talent and ask for help in developing your talent to benefit your career and your organization.

It is important to share your talent with other people. You will experience personal growth and may help others grow, too. Sharing can also be a boost to your and others' self-esteem.

If you are a supervisor, take note of your employees' talents. Have employees assess their professional strengths and develop those talents through training, mentoring, and coaching. Evaluate their progress.

Use your natural talent to improve yourself and the lives of others.

75.
Take Care of Problems Immediately

Are you a decision-maker? Do you resolve problems quickly or allow them to continue until they become even more complicated and difficult to solve?

Keep the lines of communication open. Go to the source of the problem to be sure you are putting your energy in the right place when seeking a resolution.

What do you do when you have to make important decisions? Do you research all the facts? Do you analyze the problem? Do you brainstorm ideas and solutions? Do you set a deadline for resolving the situation and immediately work toward a solution? Answering yes to these questions indicates you are on the right course.

On the other hand, are you the type who hides and hopes the problem will disappear? Some people ignore problems, hoping they will go away. This is usually a mistake. Minor annoyances may resolve themselves, but true problems rarely do. It is best to address problems at their onset to keep them from mounting.

Suppose you try a solution and it does not work. How do you react? Do you give up or try another approach? In solving problems, the best approach is to keep analyzing and trying solutions until you either find something that works or have exhausted all options.

Confront any fears you have about choosing an appropriate solution. Sometimes you have to make a judgment call. After weighing all the facts and the risks involved with the resolutions you propose, choose one and implement it. If your decision turns out to be wrong, learn from it and move on. Try something else.

Analyze problems and resolve them immediately.

76.

Be Accountable for Your Actions

Lack of accountability leads to unproductive behavior, distractions, shirking responsibility, and the like. Do not fall into the habit of playing the blame game. It is unattractive and undermines professional reputations, including yours.

When hired to do a job, hold yourself accountable to perform the duties assigned to you to meet the goals of the company. Be accountable to your supervisor and the company by giving a good day's work. When you are assigned a task, it is your responsibility to get it done. Late and missing work causes problems for you and everyone else who depends on having those tasks completed. Eliminate excuses, show up, do what you need to do, and do not stop until the work is finished.

Be accountable for your personal conduct, including interacting with others, carrying out responsibilities, and your general demeanor. Your actions should not only be legal, but ethical. Will your co-workers and supervisor approve of your behavior? Are your actions fair to everyone involved? How would you feel if someone did to you what you did to another person?

Set high standards for yourself. Follow all company procedures and policies. They are not suggestions; they are directives. They apply to everyone who works for the company.

Sometimes you will work on a project with co-workers. It is fine to want to take the initiative, but if you are unclear about the instructions you have been given, you may make a mistake. If you do, whether you misunderstood the directions or not, own up to the error and work to correct it. Claiming you did not have clear directions may indicate shortsightedness on your part for not asking for clarity sooner.

If you are ultimately responsible for the end result of a project your team is working on, you will need to follow up with everyone involved to make sure the job is completed. If someone is not doing his part, find a way to motivate him.

If you cause disruptions at work, either on purpose or by accident, cease the actions and apologize. Give the other person space. Lively interaction is one thing, but nitpicking, quarrels, and harassment are another. If you are the source of conflicts, work through them, apologize, and avoid such encounters in the future.

You may on occasion cause a problem, hurt someone's feelings, or insult another person without meaning to. In such cases, admit the transgression and apologize. Your show of accountability and explanation of the honest mistake may smooth over the situation.

Lead by example if you are a supervisor who wants subordinates to accept personal responsibility. Show your employees how they will be held accountable by making your expectations of them clear. Be sure they understand what they are supposed to do and how to do it. Provide proper training, tools, and equipment. Let them know the consequences of not completing their assignments. Then hold them accountable and implement the consequences you have set when it is warranted.

Hold yourself accountable to a high standard of conduct and performance.

77.

Be Insightful

In an ideal situation, you will be given complete information and people will say exactly what they mean. As not all situations are ideal, you may have to use insight, not logic, to understand them. For instance, a customer may tell you he does not mind waiting for service, but he is tapping his foot and has his arms crossed. He may be telling you what you want to hear, but his actions contradict his words. You may receive correspondence from a business associate that says one thing but you get the impression there is more to the story.

Take in the whole picture. When communicating with others, ask yourself the following questions:

- What is the other person actually saying in words?
- What does the tone of her message imply?
- Does her nonverbal communication reinforce her words?
- Do her words and actions make sense in this particular situation?
- Do you have any particular feelings one way or the other about the situation?
- Is there anything you can relate to this situation?
- Have you encountered similar situations?
- How do you feel this situation is likely to turn out?

Sometimes you have to rely on your feelings and inner thoughts to size up a situation and arrive at a conclusion because the facts simply do not add up.

Look beyond what you see and hear to gain an accurate assessment of a situation.

78.

Be Innovative

Innovative individuals create groundbreaking products and pioneer developments. They are always looking to the future, thinking far ahead of others. Their contributions are revolutionary; they are trailblazers.

Taking the safe road may keep you in a position but probably will not do much for your career advancement. Look for ways to offer your boss and your company something new. Innovators, often the leaders in their fields, stay one step ahead of the competition, which greatly benefits their companies.

Do not wait for change to happen at random. Think about what changes might be coming to your company or your field and use that information to your advantage.

Habitually look for ways to do your job better, assist the boss, satisfy your customers, contribute to the growth of your company, and the like. Use innovation to solve problems. What novel solutions can you bring to the table? Challenge the old ways of doing things.

Constantly update and revise your thoughts when necessary. Fixed thoughts and ideas stifle creativity and forward thinking. Challenge yourself to come up with new ideas every day. Question the way you and your co-workers do things. Is there a better way? What can you personally do better? What can you encourage others to do better? Question everything and everyone.

If you are a supervisor, establish an environment that encourages creativity. Believe your employees have incredible potential and give them room to use it. Trust they will come up with innovative ideas.

When working on teams, challenge yourself and each team member to evolve and push the boundaries. Use your collective creativity to strategize ways to streamline processes, come up with new tactics, and transform your jobs and your company. Experiment with various approaches that team members propose.

Challenge yourself to become a trailblazer and create cutting-edge developments.

79.
Be Technological

Very few jobs today are not affected by technology. Be as proficient as possible in the technological areas of your job. Keep up to date on equipment and software.

Technology is ever changing, and valued employees keep up with technological changes that affect their performance and shape their industries.

Technology can also be a detriment in the workplace if used in an ineffective way or as a distraction, detracting from an employee's work performance. Ineffective use of technology includes, but is not limited to, such practices as surfing the Internet for recreation and personal business, making or taking personal phone calls and texts, using fax machines and copiers for uses other than company business, and generally using all manner of technology to complete personal tasks instead of completing company business. Remember, too, that anything posted on social media sites is public and permanent.

Take precautions to protect yourself from email hacking. Create different passcodes for different accounts using nonsensical letter and number combinations. Change passcodes often.

The rapid expansion of technology has created a need for technology etiquette, which includes a complete array of manners specific to technology. Such manners should be heeded to maintain professionalism and proper conduct. Typical policies are discussed further in tip 101, "Use Technology Etiquette." Follow your company's procedures with regard to all aspects of technology usage.

Learn all you can about technology needed in your personal and professional life.

80.
Be Optimistic

An optimistic outlook allows people to see circumstances in a positive light and with a hopeful attitude. Optimistic people do not let setbacks overwhelm them and do not let situations or other people control their emotions.

Look at every task, project, day, week, and situation with optimism and a sense that everything is possible. Find a way to create possibilities. Anticipate opportunities.

We talk to ourselves constantly. Monitor your thoughts; choose positive ones. Positive self-talk will help you to concentrate on what is promising, which in turn will empower you to change circumstances for the better. Counteract any negative thoughts with positive ones. Use affirmations to keep your thoughts on target.

People and businesses defy the odds every single day. There is no reason not to believe you, too, can defy the odds and be successful at whatever you do.

Figure out ways to keep your optimism intact when doubt creeps in, as it is likely to do when things go wrong. Tell yourself negative circumstances are temporary and things will improve. Turn your thoughts to what you are grateful for and focus on people and things that make you happy.

Everyone has difficulties in life, but people handle them in different ways. How they manage the difficulties often leads to very different outcomes. A positive person may find a positive solution and a negative person might not.

When problems threaten, be optimistic and believe you will find a solution. Objectively assess the situation, trying to remain detached from it or the solution. Concentrate on whittling seemingly insurmountable obstacles down to size. Believe everything will work out and you will achieve success.

Do not say "won't" or "can't"; say "How will I succeed?" Look for ways to make things happen instead of letting things happen to you. Avoid saying, "It won't work" or "That's not my fault." Make it work.

Your willingness to try coupled with hopeful expectation opens doors that might have otherwise been closed because of fearful thinking. Optimists tend to arrive at solutions faster than pessimists.

Optimism is not wishful thinking. Rather, it puts people in the mindset to dedicate themselves to moving forward and taking advantage of opportunities that come their way.

Tips for building optimism include the following:

- Look on the bright side; choose to be happy.
- Surround yourself with optimistic people.
- Be thankful when things are going right.
- Believe things will work out to your benefit.
- Turn a problem into a challenge.
- Do something every day that makes you or someone else happy.

Keep hope alive for yourself and everyone with whom you work.

8

CULTIVATE WAYS TO
ENGAGE OTHERS

Even when they do not speak, people have a lot to say through their body language. This includes facial expressions, gestures, voice, and the like. Even their silence tells us something. Learn to pay attention to the signs that indicate a person's mood, attitude, and feelings. In addition, take note of what you are telling people through your own nonverbal communication.

Treat people well, gain their trust, cooperate, and do your fair share of the work to improve your connections with them. Give people the benefit of the doubt, listen to their opinions, and be encouraging.

Keep your goals and the company's goals in mind at all times and work toward that purpose with enthusiasm and the right attitude.

81.

Apologize for Wrongdoings

Let's face it: Nobody is perfect, so we may not be on our best behavior every minute of every day. In fact, we will probably have a lapse in judgment at some point in our careers that might offend others. We are bound to commit some type of minor offense or another. What we can do is to make sure our conduct is above reproach when it comes to illegal, immoral, or unethical behavior. Such wrongdoing can land us in serious trouble.

Depending on the severity of the offense, illegal and immoral wrongdoing could result in legal action, loss of a job, compulsory restitution, jail time, or repercussions against the offender's company and its management. Unethical behavior may have similar consequences, but even if it does not, it will affect those involved and should be avoided. Always conduct yourself with integrity and honor.

In the case of minor offensive behavior, if you have wronged someone personally, apologize and ask what you can do to make up for it. Even when you feel justified in your actions, unprofessional or unethical behavior on your part mars your image. Figure out a way to forgive others and forget about getting even.

You may have offended someone without realizing you were doing something wrong. Again, an apology is the best way to resolve the matter. If you were unaware you were acting inappropriately, be appreciative of knowing your mistake so you will be in a better position to find a way to correct your offense. Having realized your behavior was wrong, you can learn from the transgression and try not to repeat it.

If you know you have committed an indiscretion or misbehaved badly, the best thing you can do is admit it, apologize if necessary, and declare you will not repeat the mistake. If your transgression caused a problem for someone else or for your company, offer your ideas and assistance for rectifying the problem.

Committing wrongdoing brings with it the risk of getting caught. Misconduct may be discovered by someone who identifies the wrongdoer and his actions. Instead of taking offense, offering flimsy excuses, or blaming others, own up to it and face the consequences.

Acknowledging any wrongdoing before the boss discovers it demonstrates you hold yourself accountable for your actions. It also implies you have the best interests of the company at heart, regardless of personal sacrifice. You will most likely be disciplined or criticized for wrongdoings, even minor ones. In that event, keep your own remarks and actions professional.

Apologize for any wrongdoings and work to right the wrong.

82.

Do Your Job

Work while you are at work. Add value every day.

No matter how much you like your job, there may be times you do not want to do a specific task. It is easy to make excuses, procrastinate, and drag your feet when you have a job to do that you dread for one reason or another.

Typical excuses for not wanting to do a job include, but are not limited to, these:

- The task is unpleasant.
- You are unsure how to complete the task.
- The job seems too large.
- You are not qualified to do the task.
- You are stuck on a particular part of the job.
- Everything is going wrong with the job.
- The duties are boring.
- Team members will not help.
- You are not compatible with team members.
- You do not like the job.
- You do not see the value in doing the job.
- The job will take a long time to complete.
- Nobody appreciates what you are doing.

If you find yourself using any of these excuses, ask yourself what you can do to counteract the excuse. Is there some way you can make the job more pleasant or exciting? How can you break it down into manageable parts or become better equipped to do the job? How can you get team members more involved? Look for ways to break the excuse habit.

Everyone has the occasional bad day at work, but if you find yourself noticing there are more negatives about your job than there are positives, you need to think about what you are doing in that job. You may want to consider finding another position for which you are more suited. Why spend day after day in a job you do not want to do?

Do the job you are hired to do.

83.

Consider Other People's Opinions

Learn to appreciate people's efforts when they contribute ideas and opinions to you on a one-on-one basis or to a group during meetings or discussions. Never ridicule or disregard their viewpoints. After all, it takes courage to express thoughts and opinions to peers and supervisors, especially when several people are gathered together.

For the person making the suggestion, there is the fear someone may laugh at his idea, think it is useless, or indicate he is foolish for making such a proposal. Many people doubt themselves before and after making recommendations and could use encouragement from their peers.

Considering another person's opinion does not mean you automatically accept what he has to say as fact or a workable plan. If you feel the suggestion presented will not work, let the person making it know why you believe it is impracticable. Be professional in your approach. Having the ability to back up your claim with facts and figures will yield an unbiased view. If you have no supporting facts and are merely expressing your opinion about the suggestion, do so in a calm, rational manner. Always criticize kindly.

You will find it hard to take someone's opinion seriously if that person is opinionated about everything. Deal with each connection with this person on an individual basis. For instance, do not automatically tune him out because you know from the past his viewpoints have been impractical. Consider that this particular idea may have merit. You do not want to lose a workable concept just because you have your mind made up against him. This may be the one time his idea is practical.

When you do agree that someone's opinion will lead to a workable concept, give him credit for the idea.

Hear people out before making a judgment.

84.

Pay Attention to Your Body Language

People can determine much from your nonverbal language. They size you up quickly whether consciously or subconsciously. The problem is they may not be correct in their assumption. This could be because you are sending conflicting signals. Your actions do not match up with what you are saying.

To come across as an approachable professional and prevent others from misreading your nonverbal communication, practice open, friendly body language. Greet all customers with a smile. Use a cheerful, enthusiastic tone of voice and make eye contact.

Facial expressions communicate a lot. With your face, you could be telling someone you are happy or sad, angry or peaceful, and much more. A sincere smile will be hard for anyone to find fault with. Make yours a winner.

Proper eye contact communicates many things. Think about the range of emotions your eye contact expresses—interest, hedging, attraction, hostility, confrontation, happiness, etc. You will want to look at people when you speak to them to gain their trust. Avoiding eye contact may signal you are hedging or being dishonest or that you are painfully shy. However, do not stare intently, as that may be considered rude and intimidate the person to whom you are speaking.

How you say something adds much to the conversation. Is your tone welcoming? Do you sound irritated or angry? Does your tone seem insincere? Is your voice full of enthusiasm? Do you sound tired or bored? Can the listener hear you? Tones can signal everything from confidence and interest to sarcasm and irritation. Make sure your tone is warm and sincere. As for your voice, speak at a normal volume and pace—not too loud or soft, and not too fast or slow. Pay particular attention to diction.

Your posture could give someone the impression you are open to what they are saying or are closed off, having made up your mind against them—for example, open arms as opposed to crossed ones and pursed lips as opposed to a smile. Your posture can also convey confidence, arrogance, or concern and caring. Stiff shoulders and torsos exude tension, whereas a relaxed posture has a calmness about it.

As discussed in Tip 60, "Be Tolerant of Others' Beliefs and Cultural Differences," gestures have a wide range of meanings depending on the culture involved and the situation. In addition, various forms of touch send messages, good and bad. A tap on the shoulder or a slap on the back convey different meanings, as do a weak and a strong handshake.

Physical space can be a form of nonverbal communication as well. Standing too near someone could be an invasion of his personal space depending on the situation, the people involved, and the cultural context.

Everything you do has meaning, as does how you say things. Make your nonverbal language speak positively.

Positive nonverbal behavior includes the following:

- Making appropriate eye contact
- Smiling
- Speaking in a warm, friendly tone
- Watching your volume and speaking rate
- Using proper inflection
- Carrying yourself confidently
- Expressing interest
- Using appropriate gestures
- Avoiding nervous gestures
- Maintaining an appropriate space
- Being cautious with physical contact
- Maintaining an open stance
- Relaxing
- Dressing professionally
- Sitting appropriately
- Nodding in agreement
- Matching your words and body language
- Avoiding nervous gestures such as foot tapping and finger drumming

You may be unaware that your nonverbal language is sending the wrong message. For instance, you may consider yourself a friendly person, but others may see you as overbearing or aggressive. Ask a trusted friend what she thinks you are conveying through your body language and if it typically matches your spoken language.

When communicating with others, be mindful of your nonverbal language. What is it telling them? Send the right message with your nonverbal communication.

85.

Watch for Nonverbal Cues

Just as someone can determine much from your nonverbal communication, you can learn a lot from observing someone else's body language. All the information in the previous tip regarding how others see you applies to how you see them. What are their facial expressions, eye contact, tone, gestures, posture, and touch telling you?

Pay careful attention to determine whether the person's words match his nonverbal behavior. Is his body language signaling he is not interested while his words say, "That's very interesting?" For instance, is he is looking all around the room instead of making eye contact? Or perhaps you have a customer who says she will accept the alternative solution you offer her but her frown tells you she is not accepting it willingly. That could have negative implications for future business.

When interpreting the nonverbal behavior of others, there is always the possibility that you will be inaccurate in any conclusions you draw. Look for more than one signal for a more authentic interpretation. By focusing on the whole picture—words, tone, and body language—you are more likely to interpret the message correctly, although even then you cannot be 100 percent sure.

As mentioned in the previous tip, you may not be aware of how people interpret your nonverbal language. How do you feel people react to you when you speak? Is it in a positive manner? Does it seem they are getting the message you intend?

When communicating with others, be mindful of their nonverbal language. What is it telling you? Send the right message with your nonverbal communication.

86.
Do Not Jump to Conclusions

Never make assumptions without having all the facts. Doing so makes it easy to misinterpret what is being said or done. It may cause hurt feelings, unhappy co-workers and customers, problems with the boss, lost business, and a host of other problems.

For instance, what if you see a co-worker talking to a competitor of your company? Should you assume she is being disloyal? Do you jump to the conclusion she is looking for a job with that company? Do you think she is trying to win that individual as a customer for your company? Are they merely friends?

As you can see, there could be any number of reasons for the co-worker to be talking with a competitor, and your guess could be inaccurate.

Never jump to conclusions when communicating with others. If you are not absolutely sure of what someone is asking, stating, or doing, you should request clarification or restate what you think you heard or saw. This gives the person a chance to correct you if you have misinterpreted.

When you do not completely understand instructions or directions you are given for doing a task, do not assume you can operate successfully with partial understanding or that you can figure it out as you go. Put aside any notion that the other person will think you are inept if you do not understand what is being said the first time. It is better not to presume, especially in the case of crucial information and tasks. If your assumptions are inaccurate and you do the job wrong, it may cost you and the company in time and money.

Pay attention and be sure you have all the facts before arriving at conclusions.

87.

Get Others to Cooperate

Develop interpersonal skills to get co-workers to cooperate with you. It is important to win the support and cooperation of co-workers, especially if you have mutual goals or if they can help you achieve your goals. Focus on what you have in common with others.

Lack of cooperation affects relationships and productivity. The more cooperative people are, the higher the quality and quantity of work that can be accomplished. On the other hand, uncooperative people waste their time and resources and those of everyone around them. Be accommodating and cooperative. Listen to others, share information with them, and do not whine or complain.

When dealing with an individual who does not do his work, find out if there is anything you can do to help. Show understanding and compassion. For instance, does he need more training? Does he understand what he is supposed to do and how to do it? Is he in over his head? Could it be that he does not realize he is being uncooperative or affecting other people.

If your co-worker never does her work or always has an excuse for not finishing on time, you may have to tell her you cannot help her finish because you have too much of your own work to do. If she fails to do her job properly, let the supervisor handle it. On the other hand, do not run to the supervisor and tattle on the inept co-worker, as that may be seen as juvenile.

Complainers often just want someone to listen. Let her talk about her situation and give her your undivided attention. Reserve comments unless she asks for them. If warranted, you might ask if she would like you to help brainstorm some ideas to fix her problem.

The exception to listening to a complainer is in the case of a constant complainer. You do not want to get caught up in her drama day after day. You might try changing the subject when she settles into one of her complaining periods. If she only wants to hear herself talk, tell her you have to get back to work.

Refrain from complaining yourself. Just as you do not want to hear others complain, they do not want to hear you. In addition, once a few people start complaining about something in particular, it seems many will jump in. For instance, a change in company policy may have several employees complaining about how it will affect them.

When someone argues with you, see if there is something the two of you can mutually agree on. If not, separate opinions from facts and try to resolve the situation. However, do not passively let someone else vent to your detriment.

In getting people to cooperate, it is important for you to be a team player and help others achieve their goals. Do your part. Follow through. People may be more willing to give you their best effort if they trust you will live up to your word.

If a co-worker or boss takes credit for your work, ask him to share with others that you had a hand in the work. If he does not, you may want to share the information yourself, depending on the circumstances.

Avoid being a control fanatic. Do not attempt to do everything yourself to the exclusion of other team members or to tell co-workers what to do. They will come to resent you for taking over, especially if you also try controlling them. Ask rather than demand.

Do favors for others without expecting anything in return. For instance, help an overextended co-worker with her project or offer to relieve her if she needs a quick break. You might even offer to give a co-worker a ride to and from work if her car is in the repair shop.

Be cooperative by doing your part, helping co-workers when they need it, and developing a mutual respect for others.

88.

Be Enterprising

Enterprising individuals like to be in leadership roles where they can influence and manage others. They are highly organized, multi-talented, and bold. As extroverts, they are highly social, which helps them convince others to follow them.

There is no reason to ever feel stuck in a boring, unchallenging job when you can create opportunities, learn new skills or technologies, or take on additional tasks.

Boredom takes a toll on self-worth, accuracy, and productivity. Look around and see if it is possible to grow the position you are in. Can you do more? Could you volunteer to accept additional responsibilities? Could you help a co-worker? Do you have suggestions for improving the way your tasks are carried out? Can you volunteer to be a team leader for projects?

Make yourself promotable and your job essential. Is there a way to make your job more important to your supervisor or your company? Does your position offer career-building opportunities? If an important part of your job is highly visible to management, is there a way to do the job that will make you stand out in a positive way? Can you learn a new skill that will challenge you?

Demand more from yourself and from your job.

89.

Keep It Confidential

Has anyone ever betrayed your confidence? If so, how did that make you feel? If not, how do you think you would feel if someone did? That feeling should be enough for you to keep confidential information to yourself.

Confidential information ranges from company business to client information. It encompasses any type of information regarding co-workers including personal discussions, secrets, and written information. It could even be something about you or about your boss.

Revealing information to individuals who should not have access to it could create problems for you, your company, and the person who was betrayed. Depending on the information and the circumstances, you could even be held legally responsible for divulging confidential information. At the very least, you would be ethically responsible for the transgression and its consequences.

Use discernment in what you tell others. People are often motivated to tell secrets and confidential information because they want to look important. Be sure you are not motivated by such actions. Be the type of person others will want to confide in and trust.

Avoid snooping for information or asking co-workers for details you know they are not authorized to give you.

Lack of discretion will diminish and discredit you in the eyes of others.

90.

Maintain a Clear Sense of Purpose

If you have no idea what you are doing or why you are doing it, you will have a difficult time rallying the enthusiasm needed to complete the task. When you know why you are doing a job, and it is a good reason, you may be inclined to do the job and even be enthusiastic about it. When you know how to do the job, it makes it easier to begin work, make progress, and follow up to completion.

A clear sense of purpose will help you see the value in the work you are doing so that when you face obstacles, as we all do, you will better handle them. When you have a worthwhile reason to complete the task, you will not easily give up on it. You will become an active participant by discovering what you need to do and rising to the challenge. You will not be as tempted to drift along and just let things happen at random.

Keep your eye on the final goal, but focus on each step along the way. You will be able to take note of your progress. Maintain the drive needed to reach your goal by remaining confident in your abilities and your knowledge that the job is important.

Maintaining purpose throughout a job will inspire you to achieve at a higher level.

9

ADAPT TO
PERSONALITIES
AND SITUATIONS

Sometimes we all need a little attitude adjustment if we are to connect with others in a positive way. We may have to ignore the not-so-perfect behavior of our co-workers and bosses and look the other way when something annoys us. On the other hand, there will be times when we have to stand up to aggressors for ourselves and for others with whom we work.

91.
Be Open-Minded

How do you react to new information, technology, procedures, and the like? In today's workplace, change is bound to occur and often at a rapid rate. Everyone who works will need to have an open mind toward these changes. In addition to accepting changes that occur with your job and company, you will want to expand your open-mindedness to include connecting positively with co-workers, customers, and the boss. Things will not always go your way, and you may have to work hard to maintain positive work relationships.

There are many occasions and circumstances that require you to keep an open mind. These include, but are not limited to, times when:

- You feel someone has wronged you.
- You think someone's ideas or opinions are inaccurate.
- You think your idea is the right one but the team does not.
- Your boss or a co-worker criticizes your work.
- Someone new is hired at your company.
- You have to train a new hire.
- A customer has a complaint.
- Co-workers get together and complain.
- You start a new position.
- You are assigned new duties.
- You get a new boss.
- You are passed over for a promotion.
- The company changes policies and procedures.
- Your company makes equipment changes.
- You have a falling out with a co-worker.
- Your company is bought out by another company.
- Some of your duties have been taken away from you.
- Your co-worker is promoted and is now your boss.

All of these scenarios could create a demanding situation that taxes your tolerance. You must have an accepting, broad-minded attitude to meet these challenges constructively. Learn to take things in stride rather than overreact.

Rather than make assumptions, keep an open mind about people and situations.

92.

Use Common Sense

Some people have a lot of education, skills, and technical ability, but are short on common sense. It may take them a long time to figure out how to do a simple task because they are reading too much into the instructions or are thinking too hard about how to complete it.

Try to solve your own problems before asking for help. You may be surprised how easy something is when you give it proper thought. Read and follow instructions carefully rather than jumping ahead and missing an important detail.

Use common sense when operating equipment. Safety procedures are in place for a reason. Do not let improper dress, failure to follow procedures, miscalculations, lack of caution, or silly antics cause harm to you or another person or to damage equipment.

Watch what you do and say. Consider carefully before doing or saying anything that may be deemed politically incorrect, hurtful, inaccurate, imprudent, or slanderous. Many careers have been ruined because people acted or spoke without thinking. For instance, many individuals have taken a fall after sending illicit emails and texts they thought were funny but the receiver did not.

Think about your actions and words before doing or saying something you should not.

93.

Avoid Poor Work Habits

Any number of poor work habits can sabotage your career and should be avoided. Employers want to hire conscientious, hard-working, career-minded employees who have excellent work habits. They expect employees to come to work every day prepared to do their best and to conduct themselves professionally.

To be sure you are on the right track with your career, display positive work habits. These include the following:

- Going to work every day
- Arriving on time every day
- Returning from lunch and breaks on time
- Keeping your work area neat
- Staying organized
- Managing your time
- Doing your work
- Meeting deadlines
- Maintaining accuracy
- Correcting errors
- Avoiding personal calls and texting
- Using the Internet for business purposes only
- Dressing appropriately
- Not wasting time socializing or procrastinating

Consistently show up for work ready to get the job done in a timely manner.

94.

Stand Up to Intimidators Without Being Aggressive

Intimidators have a habit of embarrassing people and displaying hostile behavior. People are certainly free to imagine get-even tactics, and the fantasy might lessen their frustration or make them feel in control temporarily, but fantasizing will not solve the problem.

Intimidators thrive on mistreating people and violating their rights, thereby eroding their self-confidence to the point they will not defend themselves. If someone criticizes you, do not allow him to belittle you or infringe on your rights. If you feel he has violated your rights, follow proper procedures to report the incident. Keep a written record of all such violations and the follow-up actions.

So you are not caught off guard by someone's abusive conduct, learn how to read the trouble signs. Common signs might include getting in your face, ranting, storming out of meetings, pounding on desks, throwing things, or any number of other signs. If you can avoid the person when you suspect an altercation is coming, do so. If there is no avoiding the person, try to interrupt the behavior in a calm, rational way. For instance, say, "Excuse me. I feel threatened by your behavior."

One way of handling an intimidator's tirade is to remain silent, ignoring the rant as much as possible. He may become more enraged if provoked. If you feel threatened, walk away, preferably where there are other people around.

Another way of dealing with an intimidator is to learn from his behavior, knowing you would not want to act like the person you cannot stand. Consider his behavior in poor taste and a sign of weak management skills. Resolve to act in the opposite way.

An intimidator wastes valuable time and energy that should be directed at solving problems. When he is in a calm state, you or your boss should discuss his attitude and how it affects you, the work, and everyone else. If the intimidator is the boss, you will have to decide if it is worth discussing his behavior, as it may affect your job or future performance reviews.

Never let anyone intimidate you.

95.
Shrug Off Rude Remarks

Often it is not worth arguing with someone about a rude remark or poor behavior. You may be better off to ignore the person and walk away. If you get into a rude remark contest, there is no telling how it might end.

Rude, obnoxious people make it their business in life to let you know what they feel is wrong with you and your work. Do not buy into their insults. They thrive on finding things wrong with other people because it makes them feel superior.

These individuals often throw subtle remarks disguised so well you are not quite sure if they are meant as an insult or not. That is how they want you to feel. For instance, the rude remark might be a joke about an error you have made, but disguised so you find it difficult to refute it without appearing as if you are overreacting.

Defend yourself by catching the rude person off guard with one of the following statements (or a similar one):

- That remark sounded a bit insulting.
- Is that a hint about something?
- Why don't you say exactly what is on your mind?
- Do you have something specific to tell me?
- What is your point?
- Are you trying to make a point?
- I'm not sure what you mean. Would you mind clarifying that statement?
- Can you be more specific?
- Are you trying to be insulting?
- Is that statement meant as an insult?

- Let me understand what you are saying. Did you mean…?
- We seem to have differing viewpoints.
- Obviously, we do not feel the same way.
- I don't understand why I am being subjected to insults.
- I consider that statement an insult.
- Are you making a suggestion?
- If you have a criticism to share, I would appreciate your handling it professionally.
- I do not feel your rude comment is appropriate and I do not appreciate it.
- That rude comment is not directed at me personally, is it?
- I deserve to be treated professionally at all times.
- I do not see the humor in that comment.
- Is that comment an attempt at humor or a criticism of my work?

If you cannot think of an appropriate comment at the time of a rude remark, you can always confront the person later and express your feelings.

Antagonizing rude people generally has little benefit. Resist the urge to fling insults of your own, as trading barbs will not result in a constructive resolution of the problem.

Handle rude comments with professionalism. Do not allow the rude person to provoke you.

96.
Adjust Your Attitude

Bring a great attitude to work. Enjoy your work or find a way to make the job more enjoyable. Maintain a positive outlook by making the best of every situation. There will always be circumstances that threaten to ruin the day. Take them in stride. Having the right attitude can give you the strength needed to face any situation.

A confident attitude will empower you and a flexible attitude will give you the means to handle unforeseen situations. A negative attitude will hinder you and create challenging, defeating circumstances. A positive attitude will make your day brighter.

If you answer yes to any of the following questions, it is time for an attitude adjustment on your part:

- Do you need an attitude adjustment?

- Are you a constant complainer or whiner?

- Are you uncooperative?

- Do you always seem to be excluded from group conversations?

- Do co-workers avoid you?

- Has the boss given you poor evaluations?

If you cannot change by yourself, enlist the help of a friend or a professional. Perhaps books on positive attitudes or a course on changing your attitude will help.

If you find yourself embroiled in arguments all the time, step back and take a look at how your actions affect everyone around you. Ask a trusted friend why he thinks you are always doing battle with someone. Is there anything specific he thinks you should change about yourself to improve your attitude? Will you be able to make the suggested change?

Do whatever you need to do to become an optimistic, cheerful, and cooperative individual. Such change must come from within.

A positive attitude will see you through many disagreeable circumstances.

97.

Deal Appropriately with Stress

Instead of stressing over someone else's bad behavior, a trying circumstance, or a difficult task, try to control your reaction to the situation by using one or more of the hundreds of ideas for reducing stress. I have listed some of them here. You will find others in articles and books on stress management.

Following are several stress-reduction techniques:

- Listen to your favorite music. (Use headphones so as not to disturb others.)
- Make your workspace comfortable and cheery.
- Do deep-breathing exercises.
- Get a good night's sleep.
- Meditate.
- Daydream.
- Share your feelings with a trusted friend.
- Exercise. Participate in sports.
- Volunteer.
- Play with a child or a pet.
- Do not overextend yourself.
- Take breaks at work.
- Have a sense of humor.
- Eat healthfully.
- Keep a journal.
- See a funny movie.
- Read.
- Take up a hobby.
- Vary your routine.
- Be optimistic. Look on the bright side.
- Tell jokes.

Manage your stress to manage your life.

98.

Maintain Safe Practices at Work

Thousands of workplace injuries occur each year. Follow all safety procedures and precautions in the workplace. Not only is it wrong to disobey company policies, but doing so could also be a violation of safety codes and could result in legal woes.

Safety equipment is dispensed to keep people safe from harm and danger. If your job requires the use of safety equipment, wear it and wear it correctly. You or your company may be fined if you do not wear proper safety equipment required by law. Worse, you or someone else could be injured.

Do not take shortcuts when operating machines. Follow proper procedures and keep safety shields and equipment in place on the machines. Improper use could cause injury to you, to others with whom you work, and to customers. The same is true when using supplies, especially chemicals and cleaners.

If you cause or see a spill, clean it up or have appropriate personnel clean it. Wet floors should be marked so people do not slip and fall. Keep walkways and stairs clear of boxes and debris. All hazardous material should be stored properly.

Lift heavy items the right way. Use ergonomic equipment and furniture to prevent repetitive stress and other types of injuries.

Follow all safety procedures and practices in the workplace.

99.
Do Not Bully Anyone in the Workplace

Bullying is a form of harassment and should not be tolerated in the workplace or anywhere else. These days, bullying has received a lot of press, and people, schools, and companies have zero tolerance for it.

Never bully anyone, whether mentally, physically, or verbally. You and your company could be held accountable for instances of bullying in the workplace, including facing legal and civil proceedings.

If you are being bullied or you witness anyone else being bullied, follow your company procedures for reporting the incident.

Support zero tolerance for bullying.

100.
Avoid Interrupting Others

Carrying on a conversation is a give-and-take process. Each person in a conversation should take a turn to have your say. When it is another person's turn to speak, allow him to do so without interruption. This courtesy should be extended whether you are speaking to the person on the phone or face to face.

It is rude and annoying to have someone finish your sentences. Keep that in mind if you are tempted to finish someone else's sentences. Allow the person to take a moment or two and think about what he wants to say. Do not finish his sentence. You may feel you know what he wants to say, but perhaps you are mistaken and will not finish his sentence correctly. If you have a preconceived idea about what he is going to say, you may not be able to hear the actual message when it is spoken. By worrying about what you are going to say instead of listening carefully, you may miss important information.

Conversations in which you have not been invited to participate could be private or confidential. The participants may not want you or anyone else to take part in their discussion. Avoid butting in on people's conversations.

Do not interrupt customers who are explaining a problem to you. Take note of the facts. After they have had their say, work toward a solution.

Be respectful of others; do not interrupt.

101.

Use Technology Etiquette

The explosion of technology in recent years has created a need for a code of behavior for those who use technology to receive or transmit information. For instance, sending emails has become such a popular mode of communication that employees could spend hours on that task alone. Having proper procedures both on the sending and receiving ends of these communications, as well as communications by fax, cell phone, and other forms, can increase proficiency. By following basic technology etiquette, you will do your part to save your company and the company you are communicating with time and money. Displaying proper etiquette will also convey courtesy and respect.

Email

Although email is an informal means of communication, business etiquette still applies. Write brief, professional messages.

Use business email for business purposes. Avoid sending jokes and personal emails. Never send junk mail. Spam and other unwanted emails are a source of irritation for the recipient, clogging mailboxes and costing valuable time to delete them. The same is true of lengthy attachments that take a long time to download.

Be sure your messages and attachments do not contain viruses that might contaminate other computers. Use caution when opening attachments from email addresses with which you are unfamiliar so your computer is not infected with a virus.

Personal or sensitive information should not be sent via email, as it may be intercepted or inadvertently read by others.

Keep these additional points in mind when sending emails:

- Write a subject line related to the email message.
- Write brief, clear messages, using business language.
- Be sure to include your name.
- Add a title or other identifying information if you prefer.
- Flag urgent email.
- Answer emails in a timely manner.
- Send emails only to those individuals who need the information.

You will find detailed information on emails in Tip 55, "Send Professional Emails."

Fax

Do not send unsolicited faxes, as they tie up the recipient's fax machine and waste paper and ink. Never send unrequested junk mail. Avoid sending a fax when an email or phone call will do. Be considerate of others when sharing a fax machine.

Company fax machines should be used for business purposes only. When sending a fax, keep these tips in mind:

- Notify the person to whom you are sending a fax.

- Use a fax cover sheet to identify the sender and his phone number, the receiver, the nature of the fax, and the number of pages.

- Keep the fax as short as possible.

- If you are sending graphs, graphics, pictures, and the like, be sure they are clear and easy to read. Dark backgrounds and watermarks make transmissions slow and the recipient's copy hard to read.

- Avoid sending confidential information via fax, especially if the fax machine is shared by several people. If you must send a confidential fax, alert the recipient so he can wait by the fax machine.

Cell Phone

Do not talk or text on cell phones while in meetings and during business situations. This is especially taboo during lunch or dinner; it is extremely rude. Also avoid reading texts, listening to voicemails, or accessing the Internet or social media during business affairs.

In emergency situations where you need to use your personal cell phone, quietly excuse yourself and take the call elsewhere.

Keep in mind that confidential information should not be discussed on cell phones. Never send texts or pictures that may place you in a compromising position in the future. They are permanent and may be used against you.

Extreme cell phone behavior should be avoided in business offices. This includes loud talking and laughing, arguing, and flirting, none of which have a place in a professional setting, as well as long and/or annoying ringtones. Do not talk on a cell phone where it might interfere with others in the workplace. Cell phones should not be used for personal or sensitive information, especially in public places.

Remember that anything you text to another person becomes a permanent record. Avoid controversial, illegal, and immoral text messages.

If you have a company cell phone for business use, be sure to limit your use of the phone to conducting company business.

It is rude and unprofessional to text or use mobile devices while in meetings or when you are conducting company business, nor should you constantly check your cell for text messages. Doing so takes your focus off the business at hand. If you have an emergency call, step outside the meeting so as not to disturb others.

When you do need to text for business, keep it professional. Make it short and avoid confusing abbreviations and emoticons. Be selective when sending business texts; they are not a proper means of communication for most situations.

Having a hands-free listening device stuck in your ear could send the message you are not giving full attention to your co-workers and customers who are present. Disconnect such devices during meetings and in business situations.

Additional information on cell phone use can be found in Tip 51, "Use Proper Phone Etiquette."

Internet

Follow your company's procedures for using the Internet. Restrict Internet use to company business when you are on company time and are using company equipment. This includes accessing the company's wireless network.

To avoid bringing viruses and other problems into your company, do not download from unfamiliar sites on the Internet. If you discover you have inadvertently downloaded a virus to your computer, alert the proper personnel.

Do not waste company time on social media sites. Avoid posting questionable material. This could accumulate into digital dirt that could follow you around and embarrass you. Never post controversial material or any material that will embarrass your co-workers, customers, or company. Such postings are unethical and may lead to litigation. They are also permanent. Even if you remove the posting, someone else may have copied the posting to his site.

This also applies to video and Web conferencing. Conduct yourself properly when being recorded, and do not record anything that could be damaging or incriminating. What you might think is a funny video may be offensive to someone else. Make sure you have proper authorization and releases before videotaping anyone.

Software

Most software is governed by licensing agreements that makes it illegal to copy or share them without proper consent. Read and adhere to the licensing agreements of all software. It is illegal to copy software unless permitted by these licensing agreements. Do not take company software home or borrow it unless it is allowed and legal to do so. If you are in charge of company software, take precautions to keep it secure.

Use proper technology etiquette in the workplace.

3 1170 00954 8607